ORSAY MUSEUM

VISITOR GUIDE

CONTENTS

HISTORICAL INTRODUCTION

CAROLINE MATHIEU

At the heart of Paris, on the left bank of the Seine River, opposite the Tuileries Gardens near the Louvre, stands Orsay Museum. Inaugurated on 9 December 1986, it is at once exceptionally well located, housed in an extremely original building – a former train station –, and offers a collection of masterpieces of unequalled diversity.

It all started in 1810 when Napoleon I decided to have the Ministry of Foreign Affairs built on the Quai d'Orsay. The palace later became the Court of Auditors and the State Council; it was enlarged, in 1838, under Louis Philippe; and on 24 May 1871, during the violent uprising of the *Commune*, the edifice was destroyed in a fire. The cost of restoring the building to its previous use was over budget, however plans were drawn up for a Decorative Arts Museum and Rodin was even commissioned, in 1880, to sculpt *The Gates of Hell* which would certainly have created a sensation at the opening; the original plaster model is currently part of the museum's collection.

FROM TRAIN STATION TO MUSEUM

In preparation for the Exposition Universelle of 1900, the railway company (*Compagnie des chemins de fer d'Orléans*) suggested a central station be built. Three renowned architects, Émile Bernard, Victor Laloux and Lucien Magne, were called upon to design the general layout and the façade of the station; due to the proximity of such prestigious buildings as the Hôtel de Salm, the Louvre, Tuileries and Place de la Concorde, a simple metallic structure was, indeed, out of the question.

On 21 April 1898, Lucien Laloux's project was selected. Professor of Architecture at the Beaux-Arts, he had received the *Prix de Rome* scholarship in 1878; though most of his architectural achievements were in Tours, his town of birth, he had also worked on the construction of the Crédit Lyonnais Bank in Paris. The design of his train station was monumental with impressive stone façades, and included a 370 room hotel. He had drawn all the ornamentation in an elegant and eclectic style blending Louis XIV, XV an XVI periods. The decorations were undertaken by a number of officially recognized artists such as Fernand Constant, for the departure hall paintings; Gabriel Ferrier produced the *Allegory on the Cycles of Time*, and Benjamin Constant signed *Pathways in the Sky* located in the restaurant; finally, Pierre Fritel enhanced the hotel reception room with his *Chariot of Apollo*. Three large sculptures, symbolizing the destination towns of Toulouse (by Laurent Marqueste), Bordeaux (by Jean-Baptiste Hughes) and Nantes (by Jean-Antoine Injalbert) stood watch on the façade. The central station, though already operational in May 1900, was officially inaugurated on 14th July. It was the first modern facility to boast incline planes, goods elevators for luggage and passenger lifts. It was also the first with electrified tracks, thus eliminating the production of vapor and soot and making it possible to decorate the splendid nave and vaults with sculpted and painted stucco floral motifs. Once completed it had the grandeur of the great baths or basilicas of imperial Rome.

Previous double page

View of the Impressionist Gallery.

Eventually, however, the facilities became outdated and finally the train station stopped its activities on 23 November 1939; the hotel, meanwhile, continued welcoming guests until 1973.

In the 1960s there was talk of demolition; the national railway company (SNCF) was thinking of replacing it with a luxury 1000 to 1500 room hotel. Le Corbusier, and others, even submitted top and front view drafts along with models, but finally, in 1970, authorization was given to destroy the building. As fate would have it, another crime against architecture – the destruction in 1972 of the *Halles de Baltard*, the former Parisian wholesale food market dating back to 1878 – helped reverse the decision and the station was listed, in 1973, as a protected monument and finally classified as an historical monument. The National Museum Administration suggested the building could house a collection of all the major art forms produced during the second half of the 19th and the first years of the twentieth century, thus establishing a link between the Louvre and the National Museum of Modern Art. The idea was agreed to by Georges Pompidou, the French president at the time, and supported by the following administrations of Valéry Giscard-d'Estaing and François Mitterrand. In 1974 the museum's programming was underway; in 1978 the ACT architecture agency (Renaud Bardon, Pierre Colboc, and Jean-Paul Philippon) won the contest organized by the government. Their design moved the entrance to Rue Bellechasse, and placed the collections along the huge central nave which was cleared so as to make the most of its spaciousness; on each side of the central alley, were a series of rooms and above them galleries could be accessed on each level from the domed areas of the former station. On the attic level a gallery with zenithal lighting ran the length of the façade. The hotel reception rooms were incorporated into the design, the restaurant remained as it was. The metal

View of the Orsay
Train Station, early
twentieth century
(20th c.).

pillars and beams as well as the stuccoed ceilings by Laloux were preserved, restored and can now be fully enjoyed.

Lastly the Museum's exhibition rooms had to be designed, the materials and colours chosen, the furniture selected; another contest was launched, won in 1980 by Ms. Gae Aulenti from Italy. Since then, the museum has evolved and scenography has been rethought; subsequently the large Impressionist galleries and the Amont pavilion dedicated to Decorative Arts were remodeled, in 2011, under the supervision of Jean-Michel Wilmotte and Dominique Brard. Orsay Museum has been rejuvenated and given a new start.

COLLECTIONS

The Museum's truly original premise was to cover an extremely short – three quarters of a century only – yet highly productive period that had spawned an amazing variety of artistic genres. Defining that period with precision was not an easy task as it would have to be relevant for all the arts: painting, sculpture, decorative arts, architecture and photography.

It was finally agreed that the starting point would be the middle of the 18th century, clearly a turning point which coincided with the 1849 and 1850 Salons and the advent of Realism with Millet and Courbet; with the foundation of the Pre-Raphaelite Brotherhood in 1848; with the construction of the London Crystal Palace in 1850-1851 and that of the new Louvre started in 1852; a series of events that attested to the fundamental changes taking place in every aspect of the arts. These transformations were driven by new discoveries and the progress that ensued; indeed the first World Fairs (Exposition Universelle) – London 1851 and Paris 1855 – played an important part in promoting Eclecticism as well as a confrontation between the arts and industry. The closing date was less of a problem as the period covered by Orsay Museum was to be relayed by the Modern Art Museum.

Cross section model of the Paris Opera House, made by the Atelier in Rome under the supervision of Richard Peduzzi, 1984-1986. Plaster.

Of course these dates could not be definitive: the first rooms show a few late pieces by such prominent artists as Ingres, Delacroix, Chassérieu, Corot and Rousseau; though their work is intimately associated with the first part of the century, their influence extended well into the latter half. The entire career of Daumier, alone of his kind during his generation and a link pin between romanticism and realism, is shown from its beginning in 1830; as for the closing of the period for painting, sculpture and decorative arts, some of the artists exhibited pursued their activities well into the 20th century, as did Degas, Renoir, Monet, Maillol, Rodin and the Nabis; the architecture and photography collections (created in 1839) include the momentous times of the First World War (1914-1918) and its aftermath.

ARCHITECTURE

The architecture of Orsay Museum is undeniably a product of 19th century aesthetics and technology also, as such, illustrates the great works – initiated by Napoleon III and Baron Haussman then Prefect of Paris – which transformed the city into a modern capital. The Paris Opera House, another emblematic Second Empire edifice that was completed under the Third Republic, is also a perfect example of the architecture of those times. It was one of the largest construction projects ever launched in Paris, spanning fifteen years. It involved a whole generation of artists and durably influenced western architecture. The contest, opened in December 1860, was won by a young and unknown architect called Charles Garnier. The first stone was laid in 1862 and, in 1867, the façades were completed. Unfortunately, the 1870 war interrupted construction therefore the Opera was only inaugurated on 5th January 1875.

Richard Peduzzi designed the "Opera room" located at the back of the large central alley. It offers an overview of the monument – urban environment, architecture and decoration – through a cross section of the edifice in polychrome plaster. Visitors can therefore visualize the Opera House as it was on the 5 January 1914 inauguration, set in a 1/100 scale model of the surrounding neighbourhood. The model helps understand the difficulties Garnier was up against, as he had to insert the New Opera into a "Haussmanian" environment. Indeed, he had to compete with the height of the surrounding buildings, and manage to showcase the edifice in the narrow space allotted to him. Though Garnier did produce a perfect Second Empire and Haussmanian monument, and made do with the urban environment, he refused to comply with the architectural standards of that period. He preferred curves to straight lines, exuberant

Bird's eye view model of the neighbourhood surrounding the Opera House, made by Rémi Munier assisted by Éric de Leusse, 1984-1986. Plaster, wood, synthetic resin.

View of the Eiffel Tower, at its foot a few houses belonging to *The History of Human Housing* by Charles Garnier, cover of the Figaro Exposition newspaper, 1889.

ornamentation rather than austerity and the picturesque as opposed to regularity; he cheered the building with an array of colourful marble, green and pink porphyry, lit the façades with the shine of bronze and highlighted the rooftops with a copper cupola; generally contradicting the grey sobriety of Haussmanian buildings.

A collection of about 20,000 architectural drawings are either on permanent display or exhibited during temporary shows; they offer a stunning vision of Paris and its constant metamorphosis. The 19th century was passionately respectful of past achievements: surveys, restitutions and restorations were continually underway, public and private works were launched all over town, Paris had become a gigantic building site. The World Fairs were laboratories for architectural experimentation, anything could be tried, numerous utopic projects emerged, giving us for instance the marvelous Art Nouveau style; all these are illustrated by our collections including a few unique drawings, and such exhaustive archives as those concerning Gustave Eiffel and Hector Guimard.

DONATIONS AND ACQUISITIONS

The core of Orsay's painting and sculpture collection was provided by the Louvre Museum, the Jeu de Paume – where the Impressionist works had been grouped since 1947 – and the National Modern Art Museum, which changed its focus to Contemporary art when it was moved, in 1976, to the Centre Georges Pompidou. Landscapes and official historical or genre paintings were purchased at the Salons for the Luxembourg Museum, which was created in 1818 to exhibit contemporary artists. Still the most prestigious Realist, Impressionist and Post-impressionist pieces, the masterpieces of the Orsay collections, were for the most part donated by generous benefactors.

It was the case for *The Spring* and *The Gleaners* by Millet, which were donated respectively in 1887 and 1890, and also for the impressive Alfred Chauchard collection bequest. The son of a restaurant owner, **Alfred Chauchard** (1821-1909) founded the "Louvre Department Store", in 1854, in partnership with the Pereire brothers. When he resigned in 1885 he was a wealthy man, and spent his time living the highlife at his mansion on Avenue Velasquez and at his Longchamp estate in the Bois de Boulogne. He put his wealth to use, however, by donating to charitable institutions and buying art. Corot, Meissonier, Delacroix, Diaz, Dupré, Fromentin, Troyon and Rousseau made up the bulk of his collection. He became famous for the enormous amount he spent to purchase *The Angelus* by

CAMILLE COROT
Dance of the Nymphs,
circa 1860
Oil on canvas, 48.1 × 77.2 cm
Bequest of Alfred
Chauchard, 1909

Millet: the painting had been shipped to the United States after its acquisition by the New York American Art Association – the French government was not able to scrape together the 553,000 gold francs required to keep it on French soil – Chauchard, without hesitation, spent the 800,000 gold francs needed to bring it back. Now, *The Angelus* belongs to the national collections thanks to his 1909 bequest.

Courbet's work only entered the Louvre, in 1881, after his death; *A Funeral at Ornans* was a gift from the artist's sister. Thanks to Claude Monet's initiative – he organized a subscription – *Olympia* was the first of Manet's works to be hung at the Luxembourg in 1890. On the suggestion of a few enlightened enthu-

ÉDOUARD MANET
Vase of Peonies on a Small Piedestal, 1864
Oil on canvas, 93.3 × 70 cm
Gift of Étienne Moreau-Nélaton, 1906

siasts, including the poet Stéphane Mallarmé, the State was convinced to purchase, the following year, *Arrangement in Grey and Black* by James Mac Neil Whistler; then, in 1892, commissioned Renoir for *Young Ladies at the Piano*. In 1896, the Luxembourg museum received by bequest an exceptional group of paintings belonging to the estate of Gustave Caillbotte friend and patron of the Impressionists, the collection included works by Degas, Manet, Cézanne, Monet, Renoir, Sisley and Pissarro. The Impressionist department was further improved when Étienne Moreau-Nélaton donated his outstanding collection, including works by Manet, Monet, Pissarro and Sisley.

Étienne Moreau-Nélaton (1859-1927) was a very special patron of the Arts as he was also an artist himself and one of the leading art historians of his time. He enhanced the collection he inherited from his grandfather Adolphe Moreau by adding works from the 1850s and started collecting the works of Impressionists. In 1906, he was honored for having given the Louvre the largest donation ever of 19th century works: a hundred paintings – thirty-seven Corot, eleven Delacroix, and pieces by Decamps, Géricault, Daumier, Puvis de Chavannes, Manet, Monet, Fantin-Latour as well as paintings by Denis, Helleu, Besnard, Maillol and Carrière –, an exceptional collection of watercolours and drawings – about three thousand folios, a hundred sketch books and quite a few autographs – including six hundred by Millet – bequeathed in 1927. He also left the National Library a considerable amount of engravings and documents relating to the artists he had studied. While Orsay presents a general overview of Moreau-Nélaton's collection, the Louvre has several rooms more specifically dedicated to the 1850 school.

In 1911, **Count Isaac de Camondo** (1851-1911) bequeathed a splendid collection with works by Degas, Monet, as well as the very first Van Gogh and Toulouse Lautrec works to enter the Museum collection.

A banker, son of a banker, Isaac de Camondo is one of the first great Impressionist collectors. Isaac started collecting young, in 1866. He was encouraged by his father Abraham who lived in Paris, Rue Monceau. His collection reveals an extremely eclectic taste as it groups medieval and Renaissance works, a large amount of Japanese prints now at the Guimet Museum, and an impressive ensemble of furniture, tapestries, art objects and ceramics from the 18th century. Among the sixty-two paintings of his collection, one of the largest donated to the Louvre, works by Cézanne, Degas, Manet, Monet, Sisley and Toulouse-Lautrec to which were added drawings by Ingres and Delacroix and

EDGAR DEGAS
The tub, 1886
Pastel on cardboard,
60 × 83 cm
Bequest of Count Isaac
de Camondo, 1911

Impressionist pieces by such artists as Degas and Manet. Though the donation was announced in 1909 – the collection was, as wished by the donator, exhibited at the Louvre for fifty years before being shared out – it was only received in 1912.

These collections were completed by that of Antonin Personnaz which comprised works by Monet, Pissarro, and Toulouse-Lautrec. Finally Van Gogh made a strong entrance with pieces donated by his friend Doctor Gachet.

A number of movements emerged as a reaction to Impressionism – the Pont-Aven school, Neo-impressionism –, these movements are also represented thanks to donations of major works such as *The Circus* by Seurat bequeathed by the American collector John Quinn, and pieces by Cross, Signac and Van Rysselberghe donated by Signac's daughter. In order to include foreign artists in the collections an effort was made to purchase several important pieces by Klimt, Munch, Hodler, Burne-Jones, Khnopff, Mondrian, Giovanni Giacometti and Cuno Amiet.

Besides the Museum's purchases (*The Magpie* by Monet; *Berthe Morisot with a Bouquet of Violets* by Manet; *The Yellow Christ*, a self-portrait by Gauguin; *A Portrait of Yvonne Lerolle* by Maurice Denis) and the sumptuous gifts received, the museum has also benefitted from the "dation" legislation that authorizes art donations to settle inheritance taxes. This procedure brought into the collections such famous pieces as *The Trout* and *The Origin of the World* by Courbet, *The Bullfight* and *Rochefort's Escape* by Manet, *Rue Montorgueil* by Monet, *Dance in Town* by Renoir, *The Poplars* by Monet, *Green Trees* by Maurice Denis and more. Private generosity has been consistent as proved recently by the outstanding donation made by Philippe Meyer in 2000, consisting of paintings by Boudin, Fantin-Latour, Manet, Degas, Cézanne, Monet, Seurat, Bonnard, Vuillard and Mondrian. Son of André Meyer a banker who immigrated to the Unites States in 1939, **Philippe Meyer** (1925-2007) became a collector and a patron of the arts following his father's example. Just as passionate about his medical practice as he was about his collection, he began building his exceptional collection in the 1980s – with Cézanne, Manet, Vuillard, Bonnard etc. – , and often purchased masterpieces abroad only to return them

PAUL SÉRUSIER
The Talisman, 1888
Oil on wood, 27 × 21.5 cm
Purchased thanks to the
generous contribution
of Philippe Meyer through
the Lutèce Foundation, 1985

to French museums with an anonymous donation in 2000. Through his insightful love of art he also met many writers and poets, and was the first to discover Giacometti and Tal Coat, then Marquet, young Mondrian, Morandi and Fautrier. Philippe Meyer's generosity was yet further demonstrated when he helped purchase several additional pieces: *The Talisman* by Sérusier, *Intimacy* by Bonnard, *Young Boy with a Dog* by Renoir, *Yellow Christ* by Gauguin, *Variations in Violet and Green* by Whistler, *Rest* by Hammershoi, *Galatea* by Gustave Moreau and *Deep Winter* by Cuno Amiet. He continued by contributing generously to the heritage fund enabling the purchase of Édouard Manet's *Berthe Morisot with a Bouquet of Violets*. Most of his collection is exhibited in a room bearing his name at Orsay Museum, but some pieces are at the Aix-en-Provence Granet Museum, at the Unterlinden Museum in Colmar, at the Modern art Museum in Grenoble and at the Fine Arts museums of Rennes and Quimper.

In January 2011, Orsay, while continuing its purchases, received yet another large donation of some fifty pieces by Pierre Bonnard and Édouard Vuillard confirming the renewed enthusiasm generated by and the intense activity of the Museum.

SCULPTURE

The extensive sculpture collection of Orsay Museum, and the prominent place it has been given, is quite unique in comparison with other international institutions. Indeed, in most museums sculptures receive much less consideration, while here they are spread throughout the most prestigious sections as well as in adjacent rooms and enable viewers to comprehend how their perspective echoes that of the paintings on the walls. This interplay challenges the dominant role consistently given to two-dimensional work and does away with preconceived notions of timelines and lineage.

Beneath the towering vaults, the works displayed along the central alley offer a valuable overview of statuary art from 1845 to 1880. More recent works, such as pieces by Rodin and Gauguin as well as Bourdelle and Maillol, are displayed on the upper levels. As no permanent exhibits can be definitive displays are subject to change. The scope of the collection and the numerous additions made through purchases and donations feed our major theme related exhibitions. Past shows include: "Charles Cordier" (2004), "Masks" (2008) and "Leaving Rodin Behind?" (2009).

The 19th century was indeed a period of statue-mania. Statues commissioned by the Second Empire and the Third Republic were used as instruments of power and coercion, they were produced on every occasion, to promote some leading figure, commemorate important events, to dictate values, to teach, to communicate. Consequently, in order to emancipate themselves from the weight of institutions, artists soon began abandoning rigid academic canons to follow new paths. Sculpture was no longer confined to city squares, façades and walls, official reception rooms and commemorative monuments, new trends and plastic approaches were being investigated.

It is the history of this artistic evolution that the two thousand two hundred piece strong Orsay collection intends to tell. A history made up of sculpture in the round, low-relief, medallions, works in bronze, marble, plaster, terracotta, stoneware or wax. Its main chapters – Classicism, Romanticism, Eclecticism, Realism, Symbolism – are certainly not sealed off from one another; they are travelled by common influences as well as by a variety of individual styles, the sum of which provide all the necessary ingredients to ensure that the art of sculpture is not, as complained Baudelaire, ever "boring"..   Colin Lemoine

View of the central vault with, in the foreground, *The Four Parts of the World Holding the Celestial Sphere* (1868-1872), by Jean-Baptiste Carpeaux.

Academisms

SCULPTURE

During the effervescent years of the 19th century, nothing was straightforward. Numerous artistic movements coexisted and styles often mixed and crossbred. Therefore, gathering under a same heading so many dissimilar works, products of distinct histories and individual motivations is not an easy task. Moreover, categories and "isms" set artificial barriers to separate shifting and complex inclinations, and are merely an attempt at organizing inconformities with the hope of finding some sort of harmony at a particularly tumultuous period in time.

A number of artists found a source of inspiration in ancient subjects, and contributed to the durability of academic models through their neoclassical aesthetics. Marble, the noblest of stones, and its inherent reference to Ancient art, was favoured by sculptors inclined to carving mythological subjects. Nudity could not be lascivious; emotions were interiorized and should not be expressed. Acclaimed by the powers that be and despite the many changes in govern-ments that occurred during the 19th century, these artists shared a fascination for Antiquity, admired Canova, respected academic models and the "Grand Manner" championed by the almighty Fine Arts Academy.

Several orientations, however, cohabited within this vast academic body. There were those sculptors who pledged allegiance to an austere, even severe, orthodox neoclassicism (Pierre-Jules Cavelier, Eugène Guillaume), while others used the coolness of marble to express either a penchant for realism (Alexandre Falguière), or romanticism, sometimes tinged with sensuality (Benjamin Spence) sometimes melancholic (James Pradier).

Suffice to say that Academism was diverse and multifaceted; it is not easily defined by words or situated in time, the artists' backgrounds and careers were indeed so distinct that when taking in the central alley of Orsay Museum, one can sense their multiple voices rising in counterpoint.

PIERRE JULES CAVELIER
Cornelia Mother of the Gracchi, **1861**
Marble, 171 × 121 × 127 cm
Acquisition, 1986

→ Cornelia is watching over her "jewels", that is to say her two healthy children and the future tribunes Caius and Tiberius Gracchus. The archeological accuracy of this group, by Pierre-Jules Cavelier (1814-1894), boasts a typically neoclassical frontal and pyramidal composition.

ALEXANDRE FALGUIÈRE
Tarcisius, a Chrisitan Martyr, **1868**
Marble, 64.5 × 140.7 × 59.9 cm
Acquisition, 1867

→ When he sculpted the young Christian martyr, who was lapidated by the pagans because of his faith, Alexander Falguière (1831-1900) looked to early Christian and neoclassical works. However, as he also wished to produce a realist representation of the boy's body, he used the photograph of a young model.

JAMES PRADIER
Sappho, 1852
Marble, 118 × 67 × 120 cm
Acquisition, 1852

→ James Pradier (1790-1852) shows the Greek poetess Sappho in a reflective mood, her hands
clasped around her knees and head bowing, she has discarded her lyre. Though the folds
of her gown are a little rigid her body seems vibrant with life.
The artist has chosen here a theme from Antiquity, still he has clearly expressed a baneful,
Romanesque, even romantic event: Sappho has been rejected by her lover and appears
to be contemplating suicide. Strangely enough when, during the 1852 Salon, Pradier suddenly
died, Sappho was covered with a black veil.

Romanticisms

SCULPTURE

Though romantic sculpture is a reaction to classical aesthetics it is not by any means its opposite. Quite a few academic artists, such as James Pradier and Benjamin Spence, had in fact coloured their work with romantic features. Furthermore, the development of romantic painting and sculpture was not at all simultaneous. Painting led the way, as indeed it is, from both a theoretical and a practical point of view, a much more flexible media. *The Raft of the Medusa* (1819) by Géricault was the first important milestone for romanticism in painting. In statuary art the movement only reached its apogee in 1831 when works by Antoine Barye, Henry de Triqueti and Antonin Moine were entered in the Salon.

The motto of the movement, as expressed by Victor Hugo in *Cromwell* (1827) sounds like an exhortation: "Tragedy is therefore today's poetry; tragedy is rooted in reality; the sublime and the grotesque are what reality is made of, they both intersect in tragedy as they do in life and during the creative act. Indeed real poetry, accomplished poetry is made up of the harmony of opposites."

Art is consequently the result of contrast and should celebrate the sublime and the grotesque, beauty and ugliness, laughter and tears. Romanticism is fundamentally different from the classical standards of balance, restraint and moderation; the romantic sculptor tangles with passion, even excess, formal disproportion and powerful stylistic features must be inherent to the subject. Auguste Préault's emblematic low-relief *Slaughter* (1834-1850) was one of his many works to be censured by the academic jury of the Salon – which did its best to snuff out any potential polemists.

Opinions were encouraged, strong spirits were sought after, and personalities were fiery. Artists were no longer satisfied by suitability; they wished to bare the soul as is apparent in Barye's animal sculptures and the epic energy that travels the very patriotic "*La Marseillaise*" (1836) by François Rude. The Middle-Ages and the Renaissance, with their treasure trove of edifying stories full of heroic citizens and broken destinies – Jeanne d'Arc as well as Paolo and Francesca (Antoine Ettex, Auguste Rodin) – are a favourite source of inspiration. To close, here is Baudelaire's definition: "Romanticism is not characterized by the subject chosen, nor has it anything to do with truth; it is simply something to be felt."

AUGUSTE PRÉAULT
Ophelia, 1876
Bronze, 75 × 200 × 20 cm
Acquisition, 1982

→ William Shakespeare's writings often inspired the artists of the romantic generation, as it did for this magnificent relief representing young Ophelia drowned, after her heart was broken by Hamlet. Her tragic death allowed the sculptor to express, in a rather sensual manner, a Fatal and a Beautiful story. The funerary plaque by Auguste Préault (1809-1879), reveals his exceptional craftsmanship as shown by his rendering of the lifeless body and the veils that enshroud it, gently moving with the flow of the river; an iconic figure of romantic sculpture.

PIERRE DAVID D'ANGERS
Johann Wolfgang von Goethe, 1829-1831
Plaster, 83 × 58 × 51 cm
Bequest, David d'Angers, 1857;
deposit of the Saumur Museum, 1986

→ David d'Angers (1788-1856) is a romantic sculptor par excellence. He produced several effigies of his contemporaries that now constitute quite an astonishing gallery of great men. In 1829 he travelled to Weimar to meet with the German poet Goethe, after which he modeled this brilliant and unique piece. The thick hair, firm mouth and high furrowed brow portray the man and his personality. The head expresses the confrontation between poise and emotion; one can sense the storm of passionate ideas churning inside.

ANTOINE LOUIS BARYE
Seated Lion, 1847
Plaster model and lacquer gum,
200 × 85 × 186 cm
Gift of J. Zoubaloff, 1914; loan of the Louvre Museum, 1986

→ From Géricault to Delacroix, wild cats have been a favourite with romantic artists. Here, contrary to the sculptures that made his fame – namely the *Lion with a Snake* (1832) at the Tuileries, which is the counterpart of this *Seated Lion* – Antoine-Louis Barye (1795-1875) has chosen not to represent the beast in action, instead it is quiet almost solemn.

SCULPTURE

ERNEST MEISSONIER
The Traveler, 1878-1890
Wax, cloth and leather, 47.8 × 60 × 39.5 cm
Gift of M. Pasquier, 1984

→ Ernest Meissonier (1815-1891) created,
as did Gustave Moreau, several little known
wax sculptures. These could have been sketches
made prior to his paintings or they could have been
produced afterwards. The meticulous detail work
supports the underlying idea: Napoleon bracing
himself against the freezing windy weather evoking
the burden of his fate.

FRANÇOIS RUDE
The Patriotic Spirit, also called
La Marseillaise, 1898
Plaster high relief, 224 × 196 × 90 cm
Commissioned by Dijon city council, 1887;
deposited at Orsay Museum, 1898

→ This piece is an 1898 mould
of the indelible *Patriotic Spirit* that
François Rude (1784-1855) produced
in 1836 for the Arch of Triumph.
This emblematic figure of
international statuary is placed
at the top of the group called
The Departure of the Volunteers
signed by him on the Arch, at the
Place de l'Étoile, in Paris. The figure's
mouth is open to call out and rally
both the reckless and the indecisive;
and lead them into combat to
reinforce the troops at battle.
This sculpture is a perfect example
of the author's intentions: self-
evident construction, dramatic
tension, expressive features.
A truly heroic piece.

Eclecticisms

The fate of a word can sometimes corrupt the subtleties of a language, eclecticism for instance is commonly used and has come to mean at best heterogeneity, at worst a mess, and ended up tinged with a derogatory note. Indeed, for Eugène Delacroix it implies a watered down notion of harmony that plagues French taste: "It is a pretentious word that philosophers of this century have introduced and is well-suited to describe the pale efforts of certain schools of thought. One could say that eclecticism serves as the French banner par excellence. By reconciling the extremes and striving to mitigate any conflicting issues their works are consequently less striking. Their language is therefore intellectual rather than emotional."

It would appear in other words that, since the movement is believed to simply be a collage of several distinct orientations, artistic indecision would characterise it best; still when looking into the origins of the word "eclectic", the act of making choices is clearly stated. Indeed, with regard to the numerous discoveries that occurred during the Second Empire, making choices was mandatory. Archeology, for instance, had rekindled the interest for polychromy (Charles Cordier), Academism insisted on exact anatomy (Antonin Mercié), Romanticism approved spirited movement (Emmanuel Frémiet), and Orientalism found endless inspiration in faraway places (Théodore Rivière).

Without careful observation it was no doubt quite difficult to find the common ground between *The Winner of the Cock fight* (1864) by Alexandre Falguière, *The Human Comedy Mask* (1859-1876) by Ernest Christophe and *Nature Unveiling Herself to Science* (1899) by Ernest Barrias. However several federating features make it possible to bring them together under a single banner: an inclination toward allegory, a great talent for illusionism, and a naturalist approach. Thus the Opera House built by Charles Garnier, an eclectic monument par excellence, is consistent with the true meaning of the word, and the unique synthetic art of Jean-Baptiste Carpeaux embodies it through sculpture.

AUGUSTE CLÉSINGER
Woman Bitten by a Snake, 1847
Marble, 56.5 × 180 × 70 cm
Acquisition, 1931

→ This sculpture by Auguste Clésinger (1814-1883) created a sensation at the memorable 1847 Salon; it was made from a life-cast of the body of Apolline Sabatier, Baudelaire's muse. Indeed, it is difficult to decide, when contemplating this disturbing, therefore heretical piece, whether the snakebite was painful or pleasurable.

JEAN-BAPTISTE CARPEAUX
Dance, 1865-1869
Original plaster model, 232 × 148 × 111.5 cm
Acquisition, 1889

→ Though it might seem quite innocent today, *Dance* caused a scandal when it was unveiled in 1869 on the façade of the Garnier Opera House. Despite their obvious gracefulness many visitors were shocked by these dancing bacchanals; one of them even threw a bottle of black ink onto the ungodly group. These critics were clearly oblivious of the genius of Jean-Baptiste Carpeaux (1827-1875), his masterful art of movement, his innovative approach to baroque models, and his impetuous, though academic, sculpting – academic notably for the use of a triangular composition. The original stone group, part of the Orsay collection, was replaced in 1963 by a copy.

CHARLES CORDIER
Negro from the Soudan, 1856-1857
Bronze and onyx on a pedestal of Vosges porphyry, 96 × 66 × 36 cm
Acquisition, 1857

→ The model for this striking polychrome sculpture was an emancipated slave encountered during a festival in Algiers. The diversity of the materials – bronze, marble, onyx – chosen by Charles Cordier (1827-1905) contributes to rendering the model's solemn posture which resembles that of antique imperial figures.

Realisms

In comparison with the other trends that flourished during the 19th century, Realism is quite easily identified. First Realism can be accurately dated as, though the movement appeared in the late 1930s, its voice became loud and clear after the 1848 Revolution to which it is inextricably linked. The ideas that support it are well documented; indeed several writers have extensively developed the doctrine in fundamental publications such as *Le Réalisme* (1857) by Jules Champfleury. Lastly, the formal codes of the movement relish in representing the world as it is, without compromising; its prettiness and tenderness (Alexandre Charpentier) as well as its ugliness and misery (Jules Desbois).

Similarly to Gustave Courbet in painting, realist sculptors found their subjects in everyday life magnifying them by giving them, if not monumental, at least life-sized dimensions (Jules Dalou). From then on the mundane became a genre in its own right and representing contemporaries was an acceptable historical scene. Peasants, workers, the elderly and the destitute were invading statuary art when previously only the unique and the exceptional could qualify.

In keeping with its strong social commitment, realist sculpture captured the present and seized the moment (Henri Chapu, Henri Bouchard). Blood pulses, flesh quivers, veins bulge: every stigma left by the battle for life against death had to be shown. Each man was exemplary, every type had moral value. The hammersmith and stevedore sat across from the mother nursing her child, and the woman reading. While Honoré Daumier was producing his whimsical caricatures: *The Celebrities of the Juste Milieu* (1832-1835), Constantin Meunier recorded working life with a powerful, almost photographic, sense of actuality.

Realism intended to capture the smallest details, those often left unseen; it favoured the trivial over the spectacular. Thus Realism leads us into the private realm, opening the doors to the sanctuary of home, and speaks of confidential beauty (Edgar Degas). Realism has an eye for the truth, and for indiscretions.

HONORÉ DAUMIER
The Celebrities of the Juste Milieu: Joseph, Baron de Podenas,
alias Cunin-Gridaine, Auguste Hilarion, Count de Kératry,
Laurent Cunin, 1832-1835
Unbaked painted clay, 15.3 × 13.8 × 10.1 cm; 12.9 × 12.9 × 17.5 cm and 21.3 × 20.5 × 12.8 cm
Acquisition, 1980

→ These unbaked clay pieces are coloured with oil paint. They were rough studies made
in preparation for the lithographs Honoré Daumier (1808-1879) intended for the newspapers.
This collection of thirty six busts, which make for a delightfully satirical gallery of portraits,
aims to mock and provoke; clearly trying the limits of liberty of speech under the July Monarchy,
then in power.

CONSTANTIN MEUNIER
Antwerp Harbour Docks: Stevedore,
1890
Bronze, 48.3 × 23.5 × 18.8 cm
Acquisition, 1890

→ Here the Belgian sculptor
Constantin Meunier (1831-1905)
has represented a stevedore
whose job was to unload goods
from the ships at dock.
No superfluous details,
no narrative, just a man at work,
stripped of all worldly possessions
except for his own body. Despite
the small scale of the piece,
the starkness of this working
body produces a feeling of
monumentality. This emblematic
figure of Realism, honouring
the labourer, was celebrated
both in France and in Belgium.
Several bronzes were cast either
in life-sized format or in a smaller
version.

AIMÉ JULES DALOU
Nude Woman Reading, **1878**
Bronze, 33 × 23.3 × 34.2 cm
Bequest of Joseph Reinach, 1921

→ Nude in her armchair with just
a pair of slippers on her feet,
the woman, oblivious to the
world around her, is reading.
In another version of this piece
she has been dressed and is sitting
on a chair. Not as well-known as
his workers, Dalou's (1838-1902)
representations of women show
his taste for the 18th century
rococo style, though the pieces
are blatantly realist.

Rodinisms

The work of Rodin is so diverse it is quite impossible to define his style in one word. Indeed no single "ism" can characterize with any accuracy such a rich production. While some pieces can be seen as symbolist others are either clearly realist or travelled by expressionist features. The significance and uniqueness of his work warrant a distinct chapter in the history of sculpture, as the sculptor's talent and inventive creativity undoubtedly set him in a category of his own.

Because Rodin trained under several masters – Antoine Barye, Albert-Ernest Carrier-Belleuse and Jules Dallou – his production could have resulted in an indefinite mix of styles, it was quite the contrary. After being rejected three times by the Fine Arts Academy, he concluded that rigor-mortis had set into the institution and refused to comply with academic premises any further. His first decorative pieces, alive with ornamental inventiveness, show how difficult it was for him to stifle his statuary signature despite the controversies they caused (*The Bronze Age*, 1877-1880).

Saint John The Baptiste (1878) reveals his affection for Ancient art and his knowledge of classical works such as those of Donatello and Michael-Angelo. Still he deliberately altered shapes to better express either an idea or an emotion, ridding his work of conventional mimetic representation. By twisting bodies, separating limbs, cutting heads off and cross-breeding creatures his sculpture is a treasure trove of human animals at once sensual and brutish. With *Gates of Hell* (1880-circa 1890), the bestiary was tamed; this monumental piece synthesised the artist's genius and set the standards for generations of artists.

Rodin was in fact a mentor despite himself; he never established a method. His followers were either his students (Camille Claudel) or his executants – those who carved and chiselled under the master's supervision such as Jules Desbois, Antoine Bourdelle and Charles Despiau – some of them followed in his tracks while others branched off into their own directions. Still they all benefitted from the marvellous gift of freedom Rodin had offered them.

AUGUSTE RODIN
The Bronze Age, **1877-1880**
Bronze, 178 × 59 × 61.5 cm
Acquisition, 1880

→ When the piece was presented in 1877, Rodin's brilliant craftsmanship was actually detrimental to his work. Indeed the accuracy of the anatomy and exceptional quality of his sculpting caused sceptical minds to accuse Rodin of having made a life-cast. It took numerous testimonies and proof to the contrary for the sculpture to at last receive its much deserved recognition as a masterpiece.

AUGUSTE RODIN
Gates of Hell, **1880-circa 1890**
Plaster, 635 × 400 × 94 cm
Rodin Donation, 1916

→ *The Gates of Hell* was originally intended for the Museum of Decorative Arts, a project that was unfortunately cancelled before coming to fruition. As the piece no longer had a place to land, what was to become his aesthetic manifesto was progressively improved with a profusion of figures inspired by Dante's *Divine Comedy*. Auguste Rodin (1840-1917) experimented with a number of novel assemblages of groups and figures (*Shades, Ugolin, The Thinker*). Much copied and admired, the "Gates" became a monumental statement, definitively liberating sculpture from both academic norms and the laws of gravitation.

JULES DESBOIS
Destitution, 1884-1894
Baked clay sketch on marble base,
38.5 × 18 × 25 cm
Acquisition, 2003

→ The model – Marie Caira –
was an aged Italian woman who
also modelled for Camille Claudel
and Auguste Rodin; in this case
she inspired Jules Desbois
(1851-1935) who worked under
Rodin. The sculpture, featuring
human decrepitude, is extremely
realistic; it received public acclaim
at the 1884 Salon.

CAMILLE CLAUDEL
Maturity, 1895-1902
Bronze, 114 × 163 × 72 cm
Acquisition, 1982

→ A man – Rodin – is torn between two women. The first, the eldest, is winning. Her name is Rose, Rodin's long-time companion and future wife. Camille Claudel (1864-1943) represents herself as the abandoned mistress beseeching her lover; her extended arms seem to plead for his attention, as he strides forward without looking back. The group is conducive to meditation on aging and separation, and a magnificent technical tour de force for the extraordinary energy that travels is taut diagonal lines and stirring shapes. *Maturity* is a highly ambitious symbolist piece.

Symbolisms

SCULPTURE

Symbolist sculptors sought, first and foremost, to express that which lies between lines and shapes. The observations of the Naturalists and the sophistication of the Illusionists did not find favour with them. Rodin's breakthrough encouraged their conviction: the power of emotions should be the focus and was the only truly meaningful objective, at a time when industrialization had set the world in turmoil and materialism had become widespread. The poet Stéphane Mallarmé made it clear: "Suggesting is the ideal."

The philosophical quest for ideal ideas produced some astonishing, sometimes even strange works the sole intent of which was to communicate a powerful idea even if to do so the piece might very well lose a great deal of plausibility. The outside world was no longer a subject of interest, in its stead the artist represented a private, intimate world made of visions and oddities, convoluted shapes and bizarre lines. No narrative, no details, for these were superfluous. Symbolism, at its purest, gave birth to shapes that were reduced to their essence, even altered. As a consequence many sculptures are reminiscent of primitive styles (Paul Gauguin,

Jean Carriès), making any definitive classifying quite difficult.

A magnificent source of inspiration for symbolists was the work of Rodin who expresses with such voluptuousness his inclination for ardent passion (*Fugit Amor*, 1886). Sculptors, both French and foreign, were, meanwhile, watching. Symbolism, however, travelled far and wide, its international impact – from Norway to Italy, Belgium to Poland – was remarkable. Orsay Museum has therefore been attentive to purchasing, exhibiting and researching pieces produced by sculptors whose work was often misjudged; indeed by making their sculpture accessible, at last their artwork and itineraries can be re-evaluated.

When embracing Ferdinand Khnopff's faces – reminiscent of times immemorial – , and Boleslas's skeletal heads, while contemplating Ville Vallgren's inconsolable *Grief* (circa 1893) and Séraphin Soudbinine's *Sleeping Monsters*, the viewer is able to discover the strange, disturbing pieces of these unknown artists, and, possibly, even recognise a familiar nightmare.

GEORGES MINNE
Boy Kneeling at the Spring, circa 1898
Bronze,
78.5 × 19 × 43.5 cm
Gift of Enrique Mistler, 1933

➜ Just as Rodin had done with his *Shadows*, from *Gates to Hell*, Georges Minne (1866-1941) produced five "kneeling boys" to be set round the edge of a fountain. The emaciated figure and lean sober lines are characteristic of Belgian symbolism.

FRANZ VON STUCK
Beetoven, 1900
Plaster, 48 × 48 × 14 cm
Gift of the "Société des amis du Louvre", 1992

➜ Qualifying both as a sculpture and a painting, this hybrid piece is quite enigmatic. In order to mix idea and reality, symbol and realism, Franz von Stuck (1863-1928) was inspired by Beethoven's famous live-cast. The German composer was at the time celebrated by an entire generation of sculptors.

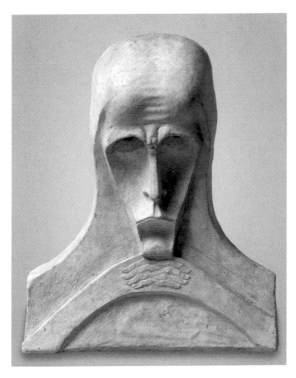

BOLESLAS BIEGAS
The Sphinx, 1902
Plaster, 46 × 39 × 11 cm
Acquisition, 1987

→ Although the Polish sculptor Boleslas Biegas (1877-1954) has been forgotten, he used to be quite an important figure. This disturbing piece, at once geometric and hieratic, reflects on how closely knit life and death are thus expressing mankind's inherently tragic destiny.

FERNAND KHNOPFF
Future, 1898
Coloured white marble, brass and copper,
45.5 × 28 × 20 cm
Acquisition, 2006

→ Fernand Khnopff (1858-1921) had his sister Marguerite pose for this diaphanous, almost virginal looking piece. The realism of the marble sculpture, highlighted with colours and wearing a laurel wreath, is abruptly interrupted by the missing top of the skull, sliced off as that of a Christian martyr. Could this androgynous figure allude to some lost love?

Modern Classicisms

On the brink of the 20th century, the world of sculpture was in turmoil. Artists were investigating new expressions, freeing themselves from the academic rules that had, just a few decades before, kept their work in check. Independence was gaining ground in the arts, lines and shapes no longer obeyed prescriptive norms, direct carving and the rediscovery of polychromy were invigorating the medium. The various yearly venues that took place at the time recorded these formal evolutions and sculpture finally seemed to have caught up with the usually more innovative domain of painting.

However this revolution could have led to a dead end. Due to the symbolist need to express ideas through form, shapes were being distorted beyond recognition. Primitivism which favoured simplistic lines and coarser techniques had lost touch with what the Old World had seen as lovely. Sculpture was now altering reality, actually deconstructing it. Soon representing reality would become irrelevant, abstraction would prevail expressing an altogether different story (Henri Gaudier-Brzeska, Constantin Brancusi).

For the moment several sculptors were intent on blending innovation and tradition. Revolution, by definition, implies revolving and the return of past things filtered through new conceptions of the world. Though many artists admired Rodin immensely, they were wary of being stifled by such a great master. A few of them worked under him, and at his side perfected their technique while learning a greater art. Others, such as Joseph Bernard, revered their elder but were never offered the opportunity to benefit from his advice. Suffice to say that they all believed they were descendants of a long lineage in which Rodin held a prominent place.

It therefore became necessary, through strong aesthetic choices, to counter all those who wished to ban past codes and start with a clean slate, as they refused to see that many contemporary masterpieces were after all a product of Ancient art. The synthetic works produced by these artists, though strongly rooted in the future, unequivocally claimed their origins. Thus Aristide Maillol drew from Antiquity a cornucopia of volumes (*Eve with the Apple*, 1899), Bourdelle borrowed from archaisms – ancient and medieval – producing novel stylisations (*The Head of Appollo*, 1900-0909), and Pompon captured the enduring monumentality and classical permanence of animal representation (*White Bear*, 1923-1933). Sculpture, indeed, remembers its past.

ANTOINE BOURDELLE
Head of Apollo, **1900-1909**
Bronze, 67.5 × 27.2 × 25.3 cm
"Dation" Dufet-Bourdelle, 1989

→ This major piece by Bourdelle marked a turning point for the artist; he has freed himself from the influence of Rodin whom he had assisted for fifteen years (1893-1908). Set on an angular base the crackled face seems to have been unearthed from some ancient time, a feeling that the astonishing mercury gilding reinforces.

JOSEPH ANTOINE BERNARD
Straining towards Nature, 1906-1907
Limestone, 32 × 29 × 31.5
Gift of Jean Bernard, 1980

→ The simple features and compact volumes of this monumental head is characteristic of Joseph Bernard (1866-1932) who practiced direct carving and sought synthetic solutions, including archaism and primitivism, tradition and innovation to obtain: modern classicism.

ARISTIDE MAILLOL
Mediterranean, 1923-1927
Marble, 110.5 × 117.5 × 68.5 cm
Acquisition, 1977

→ A symbol of Olympian shapeliness, this sculpture by Aristide Maillol (1861-1944) made quite an impression when it was exhibited at the 1905 autumn Salon. The writer André Gide coined the now famous phrase that summarized perfectly the modern the piece: "She is beautiful and meaningless".

ANTOINE BOURDELLE
*Hercules Killing the Birds
of Lake Stymphalis,* **1906-1909**
Bronze, 248 × 247 × 123 cm
Acquisition, 1924

➜ When this sculpture was
presented at the 1910 Salon,
critics were dumbfounded.
Antoine Bourdelle (1861-1929)
delivered here an unforgettable
piece; the features of the model
– the very athletic commander
Doyen-Parigot – are stylised,
yet archaic tradition is fully
respected. The absence of quiver
and string on the bow contribute
to streamlining Hercules's figure
as he hunts the birds at Lake
Stymphalis; confirming that
realism was not intended here.
The piece, reproduced several
times for a number of institutions
round the world, received
international acclaim.

Sculptures by painters

SCULPTURE

The Orsay Museum has included in its collections many pieces sculpted by artists who, because the larger part of their work was two dimensional, were considered to be painters. The fact that there were crossovers from one technique to the other was typical of the late 19th century, a time when barriers between genres were beginning to fall, and traditional values were being rejected. So if a plaster cast could be painted, then a painting could also, as Pablo Picasso's did, contain a three-dimensional object. Compartmentalisation was definitely beginning to disappear.

Edgar Degas presented his *Small Dancer Aged Fourteen* at the sixth Impressionist exhibition in 1881. It was a wax sculpture, naturally coloured, fitted with real hair, a real muslin tutu and a silk top. Critics and the public were shocked. The disturbing illusion made the viewer feel uneasy; the young girl immediately became the embodiment of perversion as expressed by her animal like features; the figure, apparently in a ballerina's attitude, with a closer look reminded of a prostitute. The piece displayed at Orsay is a bronze that was cast between 1921 and 1931.

The Monument to Gérôme (1878-1909) is a complex piece as it is the result of several *"mises en abyme"*. The painter Jean-Léon Gérôme who had painted a hyperrealist gladiator scene decided to extract two characters and produce them as life-sized sculptures. Though the group had been painstakingly documented to be archeologically exact, it was never exhibited and left to gather dust until Aimé Morot decided to incorporate it into a monument in honour of his father-in-law.

Paul Gauguin put all the wild primitivism of his paintings into *Oviri* (1894). With the help of the ceramist Ernest Chapelet, Gauguin has managed to produce textured effects by using highly symbolic stoneware to represent this pagan idol forcing evil – a she-wolf and her cub – into submission.

Whether in space or on the canvas artists were beginning to experiment with colour and volume. After all, there was little difference between a painted portrait and a sculpted portrait. As a matter of fact, the bust of *Madame Renoir* (1916) was made after a painting, following instructions given by Renoir (1841-1919) whose hands were deformed by rheumatisms and had become useless; here he counted on the marvellous touch of his docile collaborator, Richard Guino (1890-1973).

AUGUSTE RENOIR ET RICHARD GUINO
Mrs Renoir, 1916
Polychrome mortar, 82.4 × 53 × 34.5 cm
Acquisition, 1955

PAUL GAUGUIN
Oviri, 1894
Stoneware, 75 × 19 × 27 cm
Acquisition, 1987

JEAN LÉON GÉRÔME
Monument to Gérôme, or Gérôme sculpting the Gladiators, 1878-1909
Bronze, 360 × 182 × 17 cm
Acquisition, 1955

EDGAR DEGAS
Small Dancer Aged Fourteen,
the wax sculpture 1865-1881,
the bronze sculpture 1921-1931
Bronze, tulle, satin and wood, 98 × 35.2 × 24.5 cm
Acquisition, 1930

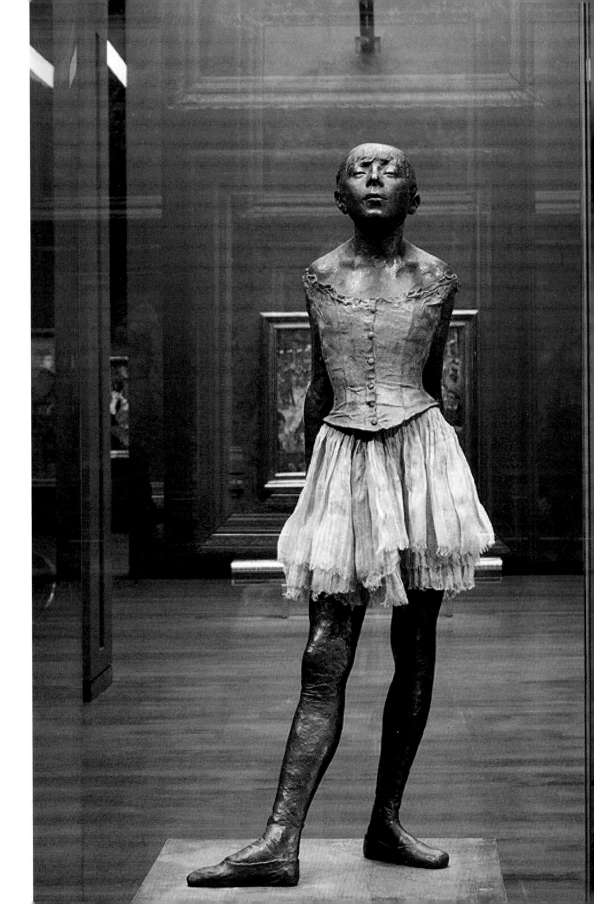

PAINTING

View of the Courbet
Room with, in the
foreground,
The Human Comedy,
or *The Masque*
(1876) and, in the
background,
A Funeral at Ornans
(1850) and *Death
of the Stag* (1867)
by Gustave Courbet.

Although the Orsay Museum is fairly recent, its collections of over five thousand exceptional paintings and graphic art pieces have bene-fitted from the history of other institutions. Its corpus offers an exten-sive overview of the history of painting from 1848 to 1914, thanks to the redistribution of the collection of living artists' works acquired for the Luxembourg Museum, the restructuring of the Jeu de Paume and Louvre museums, the prestigious collections received as donations as well as the current acquisitions policy.

Pieces from the great academic traditions – neo-Greeks, "pompièrisme" etc. –, which prevailed in the 19th century, are mixed with avant-garde movements – Realists, Impressionists, Symbolists, Nabis – and foreign schools represented by the works of Burne-Jones, Munch and Klimt. The works by Courbet, Millet and the Barbizon School, and those of their predecessors Delacroix, Ingres, Chassériau and Daumier connect the Orsay timeline with that of the Louvre, and make for the world's most extensive collection of paintings from the second half of the 19th century. The Museum rooms and galleries offer an even deeper insight into the historical movements illustrated by the works of Manet, Monet, Degas, Renoir, Bazille, Caillebotte, Pissarro and Sisley, as well as those by Cézanne, Seurat, Gauguin, the Pont-Aven school, and pieces by the Symbolists and the Nabis which are the last significant move-ments of French painting in the 1900s housed at Orsay. Such a broad variety of aesthetic choices enables the viewer to delve into the intense artistic activities of that period, and witness the conflicts, debates and questionings of those times. In addition to famous works like Manet's *Picnic*, Courbet's *Origin of the World*, Monet's series of cathedrals and Van Gogh's *Self-portrait* etc., the Museum conserves a great deal of exceptional works which though less known by the larger public deserve recognition.

Also, since the 2011 remodeling of Orsay Museum, the new distribu-tion favors a mix: paintings and drawings are assembled with other creative disciplines – sculpture, decorative arts, etc. The resonance thus created is both enriching and a feast for the eyes. Thomas Schlesser

Classicism and Academism

PAINTING

Although the 19th century was a time which gave birth to countless stylistic innovations, when the art world was driven by the romantic notion that traditions ought to be broken, classicism or the idea of formal harmony and balance still remained a founding principle. Apprentice painters were expected to acquire a sound training in and knowledge of the ancient masters acquired by copying Ancient and Renaissance masterpieces.

Most masters supported the primacy of the stable and rational line over colour and its passionate excesses. One of the leading much feared and respected figures of the French School, Jean-Auguste Dominique Ingres, declared: "the proof of the art is in the drawing", thus contradicting Eugène Delacroix's aesthetic positions. Above all, the supporters of classicism are staunch believers in the hierarchy of genres: "noble" subjects are those drawn from sacred or secular history, literature and mythology, any other topics are deemed irrelevant. Although landscapes and scenes from everyday life are increasingly present at the Salon and on the art market, Cabanel, Bougereau and Gérôme prefer monumental and historical compositions intended to both elevate the mind and impress the viewer. Their critical and commercial success was phenomenal during the latter part of the 19th century, and their works were sought after by collectors around the world, namely in the United States. Due to their recognition and status their influence on the art world was immense.

At its height Classicism borders on Academism, a school of painting that has been criticized, despite its efficiency, for being tediously conventional; overly polished with tawdry, iridescent hues and meticulous detail; and nearing a somewhat hallucinatory Verism. Nevertheless the emphatic style and almost laughable theatrics could very well be the harbinger of modern exhibitionism, even the vanguard of an imminent technological revolution: Cinematography.

JEAN LÉON GÉRÔME
Young Greeks and the Cock Fight, 1846
Oil on canvas, 143 × 204 cm
Acquisition, 1873

→ Jean Léon Gérôme (1824-1904) was quite young when this painting was exhibited at the 1847 Salon. He claimed to be a "Neo-Greek", in other words his art intended to rehabilitate the Ancient World and its ideals through his choice of subjects and a formal rendering. Light colours, clearly defined lines and grace are characteristic of Gérôme's classicism.

ALEXANDRE CABANEL
The Birth of Venus, 1863
Oil on canvas, 130 × 225 cm
Acquisition through the national
annual allowance for Napoleon III,
1863; transferred to the National
Museums, 1879

→ Napoleon III purchased this
painting by Alexandre Cabanel
(1823-1889) for an extremely
high price; it received public
acclaim during its exhibition
in 1863. Because it staged the
mythological theme of Venus
delivered by the sea, the allusive
erotic attitude of the goddess
of love was deemed appropriate
and consequently much
appreciated.

JEAN AUGUSTE DOMINIQUE INGRES
The Spring, 1856
Oil on canvas,
163 × 80 cm
Bequest by
the Countess Duchâtel,
1878; deposit of
the Louvre

→ It took
Jean-Auguste
Dominique Ingres
(1780-1867) a
lifetime to perfect
this painting.
The smooth
alabaster finish
of the skin is indeed
remarkable, and
evokes the "canons
of beauty" as seen
by Raphael, the
unsurpassable
master according to
Ingres, who sought
here to reproduce
the Italian master's
style as shown by
the natural grace,
gentle smile, fluid
silhouette and
perfect setting.

PAINTING

CORMON
Cain, 1880
Oil on canvas, 400 × 700 cm
Acquisition, 1880

→ This large painting
illustrates a biblical
theme: The clan of Cain,
the offspring of Adam
and Eve who killed his
brother Abel, is fleeing
from divine wrath. It also
investigates the primitive
origins of mankind, a topic
that Cormon (1845-1924)
researched at length
in his work.

HENRI REGNAULT
*Execution without
Judgement under
the Moorish Kings
of Granada*, 1870
Oil on canvas, 302 × 146 cm
Acquisition, 1872

→ Spectacularly framed
from a low-angle,
thus accentuating
the impressive stature
of the figure, this
classical painting by
Henri Regnault (1843-
1871) caters to western
preconceptions.
The grandiose, beautiful
Orient appears violent
and cruel as illustrated
by the executioner
towering over his victim,
beheaded without trial.
The unfortunate man's
head has rolled towards
the foreground and lies
in a pool of blood.

WILLIAM
BOUGUEREAU
Dante and Virgil in Hell,
1850
Oil on canvas, 281 × 225 cm
Acquisition by "dation"
to the State, 2010

→ This piece
by Adolphe-William
Bouguereau (1825-1905)
is inspired by Dante.
Though in keeping
with the tradition
of Academism, the
intensity of the rage
expressed in the
struggling bodies is both
audacious and original.
The monumental
proportions contribute
to the fantastic
atmosphere of the piece
which brought fame to
the twenty-five year old
painter.

THOMAS COUTURE
Decadent Romans
or *The Roman Orgy*, 1847
Oil on canvas, 472 × 772 cm
Commissioned by the State, 1846

→ This painting caused a sensation at the 1847 Salon.
Thomas Couture (1815-1879) took three years to complete
it and when it was finally exhibited the public admired it for
its impressive dimensions, its rich subject and formal balance.
The State paid 12 000 francs for its purchase – quite a large
amount – and decorated the author. The perfect distribution

of the symmetrically placed and softly light figures confirms
it as a paragon of neoclassic aesthetics. Raphael's compositions
and frescos at the Vatican immediately come to mind as well
as Veronese's immense pieces such as the *Wedding at Cana*.
Its subject, inspired by Ancient Rome, subtly opposes the tall
sombre statues – reminiscent of the glorious past – with the
drunken Romans in lustful abandon. Here Couture unites
sensual expression with cerebral idealism. Still, beyond
the artistic challenge, the painting implies a critical comment
on the decadent atmosphere under the July Monarchy,
in power at the time, which the 1848 Revolution was soon
to topple.

Orientalism

PAINTING

In the 19th century Orientalism had infiltrated all the arts: painting, literature, music... A fascination that originated in a series of political events – Bonaparte in Egypt, the Greek upheaval against the Turks, the annexation of Algeria in 1830 to name only a few – still, despite such painters as Delacroix whose work often commented on current events, the Orient was mostly seen as a wonderful and vast geographical area that spurred the imagination. It had become a perfect destination for those who wished to escape the stifling modernity that had been overwhelming the western world.

Though Ingres had never set foot there, he imagined numerous lascivious scenes that greatly influenced the work of his students as shown in Chassériau's *Tepidarium*. The erotic fantasies and latent violence carried by Orientalism was particularly appealing to the 19th century establishment.

Although extra-Europeans were often tagged with condescending stereotypes, some artists also recorded archeological and ethnographic information, illustrating with near clinical precision mores and customs, dress and physical features encountered during their extensive research trips abroad. Eugène Fromentin, who painted the terrifying *Country of Thirst*, is one of the main representatives of this trend; others are Léon Belly, who took part in a scientific mission to Lebanon, Palestine and Egypt, and Gustave Guillaumet with his spectacular piece *The Sahara* in which a magnificently lit desert serves as a backdrop for a decaying carcass.

The attraction to the Orient continued beyond the 19th century with such audacious artists as Gustave Moreau or Auguste Renoir (*The Mosque*, 1881) and in their wake Matisse, Kandinsky and many more, each exploring the topic in their own manner. The impact of oriental craftsmanship explored by the avant-gardists unleashed extraordinary energies, amazing light, and inspiring contrasts all enhancing their formal rather than narrative content.

EUGÈNE DELACROIX
The Lion Hunt, drawing, **circa 1854**
Oil on canvas, 86 × 115 cm
Acquisition, 1984

→ The Orient is a treasure trove of splendid and terrifying wild beasts and birds. In this drawing for a painting – destroyed in a fire – , by Eugène Delacroix (1798-1863), the ferocity of the lions launched into a lethal battle against the hunters, is expressed through a flamboyant palette of colours that brings strength and movement to the piece.

THÉODORE CHASSÉRIAU
The Tepidarium, 1853
Oil on canvas, 171 × 258 cm
Acquisition, 1853

→ During his travels in Algeria from May to July 1846,
Théodore Chassériau (1819-1856) produced numerous
pencil and watercolour studies recording local everyday
life scenes. This painting was a tremendous success at
the 1853 Salon, even receiving a laudatory review from
Théophile Gautier in the *La Presse* newspaper. It is a
synthesis of memories and impressions collected during
his trip – types of women, the lascivious sensuality of a
harem for instance – projected onto an Ancient subject.
Orientalism, here, has contaminated ancient Rome, as
Tepidarium was the name for the Roman baths where
the waters were lukewarm. Though Chassériau became
a master at this genre his premature death at thirty-four
deprived him from enjoying his success.

EUGÈNE FROMENTIN
Hawking in Algeria, 1863
Oil on canvas, 162.5 × 118 cm
Acquisition, 1863

→ The exceptional precision of
the drawing, warm lighting and
controlled palette shown in this
piece by Eugène Fromentin (1820-
1876), describe magnificently
the grandeur of the Orient.
This particular form of hunting by
which the hawk catches the prey –
in this case hares– was a traditional
occupation of the Algerian
aristocracy.

The 19th century intellectual and artistic world is made up of a variety of coteries and sets –as that of the Rue Royale depicted by Tissot– , in which it was important to be accepted and noticed if one wished to improve one's career and develop a proper social network. Critics and writers would hold much sought after literary encounters –as did Edmond and Jules, the Goncourt brothers, Stéphane Mallarmé and Jean Dolent among others–; painters such as Paul Chenavard were reputed for their talent at speaking in public and invited to the most prestigious clubs. Some writers such as Marcel Proust even steeped their quill into a little venom when describing the often cruel vanity of these socialites for which political inclinations, social and financial backgrounds held the most sway. A few portraitists emerged, Carolus-Duran, Jacques-Emile Blanche and Giovanni Boldini who immortalized the elegant dandies and decadent players that made up the Parisian Who's Who at the time.

The official Salon organized by the State was not involved in all this noise. A long and elaborate history provided the institution with a legitimacy that distinguished it from those small closed circles. Still the Salon's annual or bi-annual events were a showcase for many painters and sculptors who therefore had access to a large group of potential buyers; they were however strictly Parisian Salons and terribly exclusive. The happy two, selected by the highly conventional jury, were immediately attacked by a mob of disgruntled rejectees –which usually included several leading artists such as Impressionists– that contested the modalities of the selection. Under the Third Republic the official Salon, disparaged and submitted to the competition of other events organized by galleries for instance, lost a good deal of its authority.

HENRI GERVEX
Session of the Painting Jury at the Salon des Artistes Français, **1885**
Oil on canvas, 300 × 419.5 cm; Donation of Waldeck-Rousseau, 1892

➜ The Jury scene takes place at the Champs-Elysées Palace. The members of the jury are, however, not plausible as Henri Gervex (1852-1929) –also in the group– and the other participants represented in the painting were never on the same jury. The piece gave homage, albeit somewhat sarcastically, to a Salon which, all things considered, drove the heartbeat of the art world during the 19th century.

JAMES TISSOT
The Circle of Rue Royale, 1868
Oil on canvas, 175 × 281 cm
Acquisition, 2011

→ Tissot (1836-1902) portrayed,
here, the elegant members of a
prestigious Second Empire club
in a sumptuous setting: the balcony
of the Hôtel Coislin towering
above the Place de la Concorde in
Paris. Each of the twelve members
represented paid a thousand francs
towards the execution of the painting,
and a lottery was organized to select
the lucky owner. The winner
was Baron Hottinger, sitting
at the right on the couch.

GIOVANNI BOLDINI
Count Robert de Montesquiou, 1897
Oil on canvas, 155 × 82.5 cm
Donation of Henri Pinard on behalf
of Robert de Montesquiou, 1922

→ Of Italian descent, Giovanni
Boldini (1842-1931) became more
or less the official portraitist
of the fashionable elite at the end
of the 19th century; and among
them the extravagant, decadent
and inevitable dandy Robert
de Montesquiou who inspired many
a novelist, notably Marcel Proust.

Peasant Folk

Nineteenth century painting reflects the tremendous changes underway at the time – over two thirds of the population lived in the country under the Second Empire – as from 1851 to 1881, seventy-one thousand peasants were leaving farm life for the cities every year. Artists such as Millet, Daubigny and later Bastien Lepage, Constantin Meunier and Léon Lhermitte were extremely sensitive to the return of 17th century Naturalism –with the Le Nain brothers for instance– that celebrated the simple and humble life of peasants. They were intent on paying homage to the courage and self-denial of those men and women whose work fed the country. The beauty of the fields, the peaceful landscapes and the perpetuation of ancestral, sometimes mystical, practices shed a particular light on country life seen as a sort of Eden unaffected by time. The countryside was also a perfect setting for wildlife art; Rosa Bonheur, known for her temperament, and her great talent in that domain, painted, among other pieces, the admirable *Ploughing in Nivernais*. These paintings were, moreover, a comment on the pauperization of tenant farmers and small farmers. Activities such as gleaning, described by Millet, are an account of the difficult living conditions of country folk. The wealthy 19th century painting clientele might have sometimes wondered if these portrayals sought to illustrate tradition and stability or if, on the contrary, they were homage to a potentially dangerous and revolutionary part of the population. Nevertheless representations of the countryside, its small trades and rural lands, reached an historical height between 1850 and 1900. Though these masterpieces might have had, as historical documents, an effect on consciences and despite their slightly dramatic lighting, they were, first and foremost, a heartfelt and widespread manifestation of praise.

ROSA BONHEUR
Ploughing in the Nivernais Region: first dressing, 1849
Oil on canvas, 134 × 260 cm
State Purchase, 1848

➜ Commissioned by the State in 1848, the unusual format of the canvas helped illustrate the forward movement of the teams of cattle. By representing the first dressing, the purpose of which was to aerate the soil, Rosa Bonheur (1822-1899) pays homage to the powerful Charolais-Nivernais oxen and their toil.

JEAN-FRANÇOIS MILLET
L'Angelus, **1857-1859**
Oil on canvas, 55.5 × 66 cm
Bequest of Alfred Chauchard, 1910

→ Farmworkers, a man and a woman, have stopped their labour at the sound of bells ringing for the Angelus prayer. Millet (1814-1875) has represented his two figures in the foreground, giving them a monumental aspect, as they stand against a magnificently subtle hazy background; thus symbolising the virtues of rural life.

CHARLES FRANÇOIS DAUBIGNY
Harvest, **1851**
Oil on canvas, 135 × 196 cm
Acquisition, 1853

→ When the painting triumphed at the 1852 Salon, the Goncourt brothers commented, "Never has a harvest been better depicted." The artist's light coloured palette, made up of variations of yellow is contrasted with the red scarf of the woman in the foreground; Daubigny's (1817-1878) lively, dynamic touch produces a unique sense of vastness.

JEAN-FRANÇOIS MILLET
The Gleaners, 1857
Oil on canvas, 83.5 × 110 cm
Donation of Mrs. Pommery
under usufruct, 1890

→ "Born a peasant, I shall
die a peasant", declared
Millet (1814-1875) who was
a eulogist and supporter
of rural life. In this painting
the group of three
women, dressed in tatters,
gathering a few ears of
wheat left after the harvest
–gleaning –, contrast
with the idea of abundance
represented by a large farm
in the background and
a landowner, to the right,
mounted on his horse.
Millet was comparing
these poor peasant
women whose only means
are the few leftovers
they can gather, and the
ragmen of large cities.
Two women are bent over,
concentrating on their task,
while the third seems to be
relieving her back, her head
touching onto the horizon.
From a distance the scene
"resembles a religious
painting", commented
the art critic Edmond
About during the 1857
Salon. It is true that Millet,
while intent on showing
the harshness of rural life,
bathes his composition in
an almost mystical light.

The Barbizon school

In the 19th century, representing nature –its luminous landscapes, weather patterns, fauna and flora– began competing with the edifying representation of historical events. This shift had a series of consequences: in the past, all apprentice painters were expected to travel to Italy to gain inspiration from the ancient ruins and great masters of the Renaissance, but all of a sudden young artists began visiting the forest at Fontainebleau, near Paris, to hone their art and find inspiration. At least six hundred professional artists visited that area during the 19th century. The exceptional variety of sites the area offered made it a perfect "open-air studio" with a plethora of motifs to paint: the road to Chailly, the shady Solle Valley and the amazing boulders of the Trois Pignons mountain range, the Mare aux fees ("fairy pond"), the sandy trails and the rock formations of Apremont. Fontainebleau was also, a refuge, a wilderness sanctuary far from the noise of Paris and its coteries.

Barbizon itself was nothing more than a hamlet surrounded by nature; there, in 1820, François Ganne began accommodating in his humble inn, artists eager to work outdoors in the forest. The first to settle there was Caruelle d'Aligny then came Corot, Theodore Rousseau, Diaz de la Peña, Jean-François Millet and many others, some temporarily, others permanently. The growing colony ended up being given its own name: "the Barbizon school" –though the expression that was never used until after their lifetime. The leading personality of the school was Théodore Rousseau, a loner who had a mystical relationship with nature. He was rejected thirteen times by the Salon jury, until 1849 when at last he received recognition and was highly celebrated form then on throughout the Second Empire. During the second half of the 19th century Barbizon, and the nearby village of Bourron, became such a conventional destination that artists' infatuation for Fontainebleau became a joking matter. As attest the Goncourt bothers comment "Each tree [there] is a model in the middle of a circle of paint boxes!"

JULES DUPRÉ
Oak Trees and Pond,
circa 1850-1855
Oil on canvas, 102 × 84 cm
Bequest by Alfred Chauchard,
1909

➔ Oak trees in the Fontainebleau forest can often have anthropomorphic shapes, thus this piece by Jules Dupré (1811-1889) is both a portrait and a landscape. This type of pleasant yet efficient composition was a standard: a water surface, peaceful animals, a few trees and a cloud travelled sky.

THÉODORE ROUSSEAU
Avenue, Forest of L'Isle-Adam, **1849**
Oil on canvas, 101 × 82 cm
Bequest by Alfred Chauchard, 1909

→ The alley crossing the Isle Adam forest is represented as a natural temple lit by the summer sun filtering through the canopy. It is a quiet and isolated place where men and beasts alike can rest serenely. Théodore Rousseau (1812-1867) worked on the painting outdoors from the motif, perfecting it again and again, before presenting it to the 1849 Salon.

NARCISSE DIAZ DE LA PEÑA
Heights of Jean du Paris in Fontainebleau Forest, **1887**
Oil on canvas, 84 × 106 cm
Bequest of Alfred Chauchard, 1909

→ With such a clever variation of blues and greys all bordering on black, Narcisse Diaz de la Peña (1807-1876) was able to obtain an incredibly subtle light: the stormy, dense and compact clouds, setting off the scintillating clumps of trees in a sober yet dramatic manner.

Courbet's Realism

PAINTING

Throughout his career Gustave Courbet (1819-1877) was intent on painting from direct observation of nature. Refusing to work on historical allegories and idealized characters, his preferred subject matter was the society he lived in and the surrounding world. His avant-garde aesthetic premise, named Realism, was the cause of many a scandal. The notion of Beauty was the source of the controversy. Indeed Courbet, in the name of total honesty, thought nothing of representing the dullness of country life (*A Funeral at Ornans*), imperfect bodies (*The Spring*), even the most provocative and intimate parts of human anatomy (*The Origin of the world*). The artist was adamant, if the subject was true, whether beautiful or not, it deserved to be painted.

Born in the rural province of the Doubs, Courbet was attracted by Republican and Socialist ideas; his strong political positions and unconventional, even rebellious, spirit confronted the uptight social standards of the Second Empire. When, in September 1870, the weakening government was challenged, he joined the Paris Commune and fought with passion; a choice which came at a heavy cost –a trial, exile, financial and physical degradation– that he was to pay for until his death. Courbet was a wonderful landscapist, deeply attached to his place of birth. His painting technique is characterized by a rough effect –he often painted with a knife– a unique and bold color palette –he used muted even earthy tones and strong contrasts– and very original compositions in which his knowledge of Ancient art and his inclination for folk art came together.

Though Courbet's genius was never challenged by any of his students, his work had a significant impact on the advent of Impressionism and even Modern art. He often liked to say: "When I shall be dead, it must be said of me: that man never belonged to any school, church, institution or academy and most of all was never governed by any regime other than freedom."

GUSTAVE COURBET
The Wounded Man, circa **1844, retouched before 1854**
Oil on canvas, 81.5 × 97.5 cm
Acquisition, 1881

→ Gustave Courbet signed quite a few self-portraits. This painting was originally a happy love scene. However after his break up with Virginie Binet, the artist erased the female figure and added the signs of a lethal combat... Still, despite the blood, the serene features of the male figure are those of a man resting!

GUSTAVE COURBET
The Artist's Studio, also called *The Artist's Studio, a Realist Allegory that Defined a Period of Seven Years of my Art Career*, 1854-1855
Oil on canvas, 361 × 596 cm
Purchased thanks to a subscription organized by the "Société des amis du Louvre", 1920

→ In this imaginary scene, Courbet is sitting at the center painting a landscape surrounded by, on his left a group of historical figures – including Napoleon III in a poacher's outfit –, and on his right, friends and family. This very large painting is a charade, both enigmatic and polysemous and has been the object of an unbelievable amount of interpretations.

GUSTAVE COURBET
The Origin of the World, 1866
Oil on canvas, 46 × 55 cm
Acquisition by "dation", 1995

→ This extremely bold close up of a nude could have been inspired by pornographic photograph of the time. *The Origin of the World* was a clandestine piece kept secret during Courbet's lifetime. The story of the painting is quite unusual: before entering the Orsay collection, it had many owners, the first was a Turk collector, Khalil Bey, and at one point it was even purchased by Jacques Lacan, the famous psychiatrist and psychoanalyst.

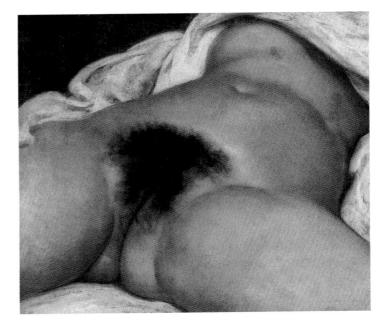

GUSTAVE COURBET
A Funeral at Ornans, also called *Painting of Human Figures, the History of a Funeral at Ornans*, 1849-1850
Oil on canvas, 315 × 668 cm
Gift of Miss Juliette Courbet, sister of the artist, 1881

→ All his life, Courbet painted the inhabitants of his birth land and its many landscapes.
It is important to note that although his representations of the geography and the everyday
life of the Doubs were, of course, the expression of his affection, they were not just anecdotic
descriptions. They were the result of crucial aesthetic choices. *A Funeral at Ornans* was, in fact,
a Realist manifesto. Produced under the difficult circumstances of a small make-shift studio, its
large-scale dimensions were similar to those usually chosen to depict a momentous historical event;
however in this scene anonymous people are burying an unknown person. It caused quite a scandal
when it was entered in the 1850-1851 Salon. Though it was criticized for its dark dirty colours,
described as ugly, brutal, sordid and vulgar, it was also praised by some, such as Sabatier-Ungher –a
follower of the social-utopist Charles Fourier– who declared that he was proud to witness
the advent of "democracy in art"...

The Origins of Impressionism

PAINTING

When Édouard Manet (1832-1883) was training at the highly academic studio of Thomas Couture, he cheekily answered his master saying: "I paint what I see and not what others would like to see, what is, rather than what is not." From the origin, the premise that prevailed in what was to be named in 1870 Impressionism, was a commitment to experience the world and nature with the utmost honesty. Without disowning classical tradition –Manet was highly influenced by Velasquez, Goya and the Italian Renaissance– they were driven by a burning desire to innovate. The younger generation of painters was intent on depicting modern society and its fast-moving mutations. In *The Painter of Modern Life*, Charles Baudelaire wrote: "Beauty consists of, an element of the eternal and invariable, how much is extremely difficult to evaluate, and an element of the relative and circumstantial made up of our times, fashions, morality and passions either all combined or taken separately." A definition that was to become a rule of thumb for Baudelaire's close friend Manet, as well as Degas and Fantin-Latour, and was later adopted by the next generation of Impressionists.

Such a change in perspective produced two consequences, for one the evolution of pictorial art in which scandalous subjects were being illustrated –*Olympia*, for instance, was a prostitute. Furthermore, Manet refused to employ any of the usual clever illusions, preferring vivid colors, strong contrasts, a visible brushstroke and large flat planes of solid colors that neutralize both volume and depth. This audacious form of expression was loudly criticized: Manet was accused of painting like a child and having forgotten such basic rules as perspective. Consequently, his modern vision and *The Picnic* were both rejected from the official Salon and ridiculed at the 1863 "Salon des Refusés" (an event that was open to those who had not been accepted by the official Salon). It became evident that, in order for painting to be renewed, other means of getting known, exhibiting and selling, had to be found; a challenge that was taken up during the 1870s by Monet, Caillebotte and all those who emulated Manet.

ÉDOUARD MANET
The Fife Player, 1866
Oil on canvas, 160 × 97 cm
Bequest of Count Isaac de Camondo, 1911

→ Impressed by Velasquez, Manet began blacking out the background, so his young fife player would standout clearly, the subject of a light infantry soldier as well as the bold artistic choices drew a compliment from Émile Zola (a leading Naturalist writer and journalist) who remarked that it showed "a real life environment both powerful and unique"; while others mocked the painting saying it looked like a playing card.

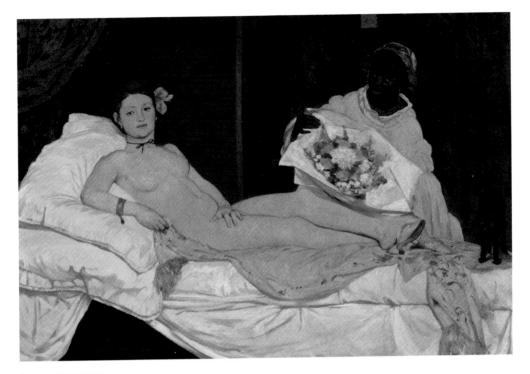

ÉDOUARD MANET
Olympia, 1863
Oil on canvas, 130 × 190 cm
Gift to the State through a subscription launched
by Claude Monet, 1890

→ Manet has reproduced here the type of
classical composition favored by Giorgione,
Titian and Velasquez: a naked Venus lying
down. However his model –Victorine
Meurent– is a prostitute to whom an admirer
has just had a bouquet delivered. A number
of erotic elements –the black cat, the jewelry,
the slipper– were added to increase the
provocative atmosphere of the piece.

ÉDOUARD MANET
The Balcony, 1868-1869
Oil on canvas, 170 × 124.5 cm
Bequest of Gustave Caillebotte, 1894

→ A painting "with no concept"
limited to "a combination of
colors" complained Paul Mantz
when he commented on the
piece. True, Manet had chosen
to paint the portrait of three close
friends –his sister-in-law and
painter Berthe Morisot, Antoine
Guillemet, a painter, and the
violinist Fanny Claus– with
no narrative or psychological
approach. The dominant features
being the subtle play between the
depth of the black background
and the contrasting brightness of
white and chrome green.

ÉDOUARD MANET
The Picnic, 1862-1863
Oil on canvas, 208 × 264.5 cm
Donation by Étienne Moreau-Nélaton,
1906

→ Manet got the idea of his
Bath –the original title of
the painting– when he saw a
group of women coming out
of the water at Argenteuil:
"Apparently I must absolutely
to do a nude. Well they shall
have one!" The composition
draws on classical works such
as *The Pastoral Concert* by
Titian, (at the time attributed to
Giorgione) and *The Judgment
of Paris*, an engraving designed
by Raphael. However, despite
the dual reference, the painting
still retained its subversive
message. The triangular
construction of this outdoors
picnic scene, crowned by a
woman bathing in a river, is both
dramatized and artificial.
To the right, the profile of
a dandy who is wearing grey
trousers, a bright colored
cravat, a cane, and a flat hat
with a pendant usually worn
indoors. He is in a conversation
with another man in a suit
while a woman –who looks like
Victorine Meurent, Manet's
muse– is staring at the viewer;
her nude body inspiring a
thousand interpretations and
fantasies. The painting was
the laughing stock of the 1863
"Salon des refusés": its style
and supposed indecency
caused a rise of aggressive
criticism.

JAMES ABBOTT MCNEILL WHISTLER
Arrangement in Grey and Black n°1, also called, *The Artist's Mother*, 1871
Oil on canvas, 144.3 × 162.5 cm
Acquisition, 1891

→ With great sobriety, this profile portrait depicts with austere simplicity the mother
of James Abbot McNeil Whistler (1834-1903) who spent most of his career in France.
The painter, rather than offering a narrative, investigates color, variations of grey,
white and black, producing an evocative dreamlike effect similar to that of music.

HENRI FANTIN-LATOUR
Homage to Delacroix, 1864
Oil on canvas, 160 × 250 cm
Donation by Étienne Moreau-Nélaton, 1906

→ Because of his free and energetic use of color, Delacroix's part in the advent of Impressionism was essential. When he died, Fantin-Latour (1863-1904), as homage, represented a group of admirers around the master's portrait. The art critic Duranty, Fantin-Latour himself, the writers Champfleury and Baudelaire, can be seen sitting from left to right, and, standing, the artists Louis Cordier, Alphonse Legros, Whistler, Manet, Braquemond and Albert de Balleroy.

HENRI FANTIN-LATOUR
A Studio at Batignolles, 1870
Oil on canvas, 204 × 273.5 cm
Acquisition, 1892

→ In keeping with the tradition of painters posing as masters, leaders of a generation and surrounded by disciples and admirers, here is Manet at his easel with, from left to right, the painters Otto Schölderer and Auguste Renoir, the critics Zacharie Astruc and Émile Zola, the art enthusiast Édmond Maître, and the two painters Frédéric Bazille and Claude Monet.

FRÉDÉRIC BAZILLE
Family Portraits, also called, *Family Reunion*, 1867
Oil on canvas, 152 × 230 cm
Acquisition with the contribution of Marc Bazille, 1905

→ Frédéric Bazille (1841-1870), whose untimely death during the 1870 war kept him from consolidating his position as one of the great names of Impressionism. In his *Family Reunion*, the intense expressions of the figures are bathed in the bright Mediterranean light that is subtly cooled by the shade of a large tree.

EUGÈNE BOUDIN
The Trouville Beach, 1864
Oil on wood, 26 × 48 cm
Donation of M. Edouardo Mollard to the National Museums, 1961

→ There are over three hundred beach scenes in the body of work produced by Boudin (1824-1898). The "master of skyscapes" exploited the formula throughout his career: fashionable beaches with a plethora of parasols, crinolines, skirts and hats; all these colorful accessories vibrating in the shimmering light of a windy day.

CLAUDE MONET
Women in the Garden, circa 1866
Oil on canvas, 255 × 205 cm
Acquisition, 1921

→ The sketchy incomplete faces are not, here, the subject of the piece, what Monet (1840-1926) is interested in is the effect of light on the vegetation and the materials. This work was partially painted outdoors, but due to its very large format –two and a half meters high– and in order to keep the same point of view when working on the upper section, Monet had a ditch cut into the ground in which the canvas was lowered.

Impressionism

PAINTING

The term of «Impressionism» was mentioned for the first time in the history of art on 25 April 1874, during a fringe exhibition of thirty-five artists at the photographer Nadar's studio, on Boulevard des Capucines. The journalist Louis Leroy quoting the title of Monet's painting –*Impression, Rising Sun*, now part of the Marmottan Monet Museum collection– said derisively: "Since I am impressed, there must be an impression in there". Thus the Impressionist group was officially born because of a quip. The artists belonging to the group had all been born around 1840 and were by then fully mature artists. Monet, Renoir, Pissarro, Sisley, Cézanne and Berthe Morisot had known each other for ten years, had shared training and formal experimentation, and had spent hours discussing art in the cafés of Batignolles and Pigalle. They had, most of all, chosen to follow their own personal path opposing official standards and consequently, in order to keep misery at bay, had mutualized their efforts and organized independent exhibitions. The 1874 art show was followed by seven others over the following twelve years.

Despite their many distinctive styles, what were the common features of this so-called "school"? Firstly, a much lighter color palette enabling livelier renditions of light. One day Renoir admitted: "One of us, at the start of his day found himself out of black, so just used blue: Impressionism was born". The most important aspects were the fragmented brush strokes which produced a feeling of movement and expressed the fleeting, changing light found in nature, in the skies and on the waters; as well as the triviality of the subjects generally painted from the motif, outdoors –except for Degas who only worked in his studio. Cézanne imagined that "with an apple" he could "amaze Paris". Towards 1874, Parisians were dumbfounded rather than amazed; still the battle was only beginning.

ALFRED SISLEY
*Louveciennes,
the Mid-hill Path,*
previously called
The Heights of Marly,
circa 1873
Oil on canvas,
38 × 46.5 cm
Bequest by Antonin
Personnaz, 1937

→ As described
by the art historian
John Rewald,
the style of Sisley
(1839-1899) is full
of "sweet lyricism".
Of English
descent, the artist
was an adept of
divisionism so that
each brushstroke
reflected light;
as a consequence
the entire surface
of the painting
shimmers from
sky to path.

PAUL CÉZANNE
House of the Hanged Man, Auvers sur Oise, 1873
Oil on canvas, 55.5 × 66.3 cm
Bequest of Count Isaac de Camondo, 1911

→ This major piece in the career of Cézanne (1839-1906), gave rise to violent mockery at the 1874 Nadar exhibition. Painted while Cézanne was in Auvers-sur-Oise with his friend and master Camille Pissarro who encouraged him to use lighter colors, the artist shows here how well he retained the lesson.

AUGUSTE RENOIR
Path through the High Grass, circa 1876-1877
Oil on canvas, 60 × 74 cm
Gift of Charles Comiot, 1926

→ The Impressionists often shared subjects and compositions as in the case of *Path through the High Grass* by Renoir (1841-1919) which refers to *Poppies* by Monet. Great friends, they both particularly enjoyed large motifs without structure, and very few details flooded with light.

CLAUDE MONET
Poppies, 1873
Oil on canvas, 50 × 65 cm
Gift of Étienne Moreau-Nélaton, 1906

→ Monet (1840-1926) wanted to render the vibrating elements of the landscape. "I want to paint the air around the bridge, the house, the boat; the beauty of the air that they are in, and that is nothing less than impossible". Impossible? The poppies sprinkled across a vast expanse of green high grass –here the complementary colors set each other off in a delicate and joyous manner– crossed by his wife Camille and his son Jean prove it was possible for him after all. The illusion actually worked, as the area was neither in the country –it was a flood zone where the sandy soil was fertilized by spate irrigation from Paris– nor was it at Argenteuil –where the artist lived at the time– but at the neighboring town of Gennevilliers. The tiny fragmented touches of color depicting the figures blend them into the landscape. In the distance the sky, travelled by thick clouds, adds to the feeling of weightlessness. "It is as if the slightest stir from nature is known to him", said Octave Moreau when talking about Monet in 1884.

PAINTING

CLAUDE MONET
The Magpie, 1868-1869
Oil on canvas, 89 × 130 cm
Acquisition, 1984

→ When the journalist
Léon Billot wrote, in 1868,
"Art has its courageous
soldiers", it was after
seeing Monet, sitting
in the freezing cold,
painting the effects
of snow outdoors!
The Magpie was produced
at a time when the artist's
style was in full bloom:
the balance, lighting
and the unique quality
of the contrast work in
his pictorial technic,
which turns whites into
blue, yellow and mauve,
have all come together in
this absolute masterpiece.

CAMILLE PISSARRO
White Frost, 1873
Oil on canvas, 65 × 93 cm
Bequest of Enriqua Alsop
on behalf of Doctor Edouardo
Mollard, 1972

→ This piece by Pissarro
(1830-1903) was one of
the landscapes entered
into the 1874 exhibition
that caused a great deal
of controversy, pitting
critics against each
other. While Louis Leroy
wrote: "it is nothing but
an accumulation of paint
scraped off the palette
and spread onto a dirty
canvas; it has neither
head nor tail, neither
top nor bottom, neither
back nor front", Philippe
Burty found the piece
comparable to "the best
of Millet".

ALFRED SISLEY
Snow at Louveciennes, 1878
Oil on canvas, 61 × 50.5 cm
Bequest of Count Isaac de Comondo, 1911

→ Sisley had a rather solitary, humble and discreet temperament therefore the sad mood
of wintery landscapes was a great inspiration for him. Furthermore he liked to deepen the
perspectives in his country scenes adding a feeling of space to the silent motionless scenery.

Modern Paris

PAINTING

During the second half of the 19th century, Paris was being rethought, transformed and modernized under the eyes of the Impressionists. Conducted by Baron Georges Eugène Haussmann, assisted by the engineer Eugène Belgrand and the landscape designer Jean-Charles Alphand, over a period of seventeen years, 60% of the French capital was reconstructed. The figures make one's head spin: 600 kilometers of sewage were put into place, and 300 kilometers of roads were cut... The renovation of the urban facilities, the many innovative technologies that flowered round the city fascinated painters: Monet signed a series on the Saint-Lazare train station and its pyramidal glass rooftop over the quays; Pissarro painted several views of the Grands Boulevards representing the incredible perspectives they offered; and Gustave Caillebotte, the perfect Parisian dandy as were Manet and Degas, depicted the charm of the bourgeois lifestyle he was so well acquainted with. Still Paris remained a city of contrasts where the elegant events of the upper class –horse races, theatre, fashion etc.– took place alongside the working classes' leisure activities such as neighborhood dances and "guinguettes" (riverside cafés where accordion bands played) and, most importantly, in an environment of dire poverty. Without dwelling on the sordid and over dramatizing, Impressionists often represented simple people, peddlers and workers, and authored many works recording the ravages of alcohol in society. Indeed they too were regular café customers –Le Guerbois, La Nouvelle Athènes, Le Rat Mort, among others –, and frequented brothels and cabarets where they explored at length, with apparent fascination, the rabble and vice of those times.

However, their geographical scope –mostly the right bank quarters– for such subjects was limited to where they and their dealers lived – from the area of the Opera House to Montmartre via Batignolles, Pigalle and the Saint-Lazare quarters. Including, now and then, a quick escapade to the Bois de Boulogne... where Haussmann had had a million trees planted.

GUSTAVE CAILLEBOTTE
The Floor Scapers, **1875**
Oil on canvas, 102 × 146.5 cm
Gift from Gustave Caillebotte's heirs, 1894

→ The impressive amount of construction launched by Haussmann generated a tremendous need for workers in Paris –5000 cabinet makers and 8000 wood workers were active for instance! Caillebotte (1848-1894) paid homage to them by painting several pieces, of a rather more realist than impressionist technique, that were rejected from the 1875 Salon for the triviality of their subject matter.

CLAUDE MONET
The Saint-Lazare Train Station, 1877
Oil on canvas, 75 × 104 cm
Bequest of Gustave Caillebotte, 1894

→ Émile Zola wrote: "Our artists must discover
the poetry of train stations." According to Jean Renoir,
son of Auguste, Monet (1840-1926) did just that and had
the cheek to ask the Station Director to stop the trains
and evacuate the quays so that he could paint the motif.

EDGAR DEGAS
In a Café, also called *Absinthe*, circa 1875-1876
Oil on canvas, 92 × 68.5 cm
Bequest of Count Isaac de Camondo, 1911

→ The actress Elle Andrée is sitting at a table,
her features bear the marks of absinthe, slightly
off center at her right, Degas (1834-1917) has
represented Marcellin Desboutins, an engraver
and well-known figure of bohemian Paris.
Absinthe, also referred to as the "green fairy"
was a popular aperitif during the 1870s before
it was banned in 1915.

PAINTING

EDGAR DEGAS
Dancers Climbing the Stairs, 1886-1890
Oil on canvas, 56.5 × 45 cm
Bequest of Count Isaac de Camondo, 1911

→ The composition of the painting is unusually drawn out in its length so as to include a diagonal perspective angling downward. The left of the scene is occupied by the ascending ballerinas emerging from the dark stairwell, getting ready for their exercises upstairs to the right, in a room flooded with light.

EDGAR DEGAS
The Opera Orchestra,
circa 1870
Oil on canvas, 56.5 × 45 cm
Donation of Miss Dihau
under usufruct, 1923

→ In this composition Degas chose an unusual and bold frame that practically eludes the dancers –their heads are truncated– to focus on the orchestra; at the center, his friend Désiré Dihau is playing the bassoon. In the back ground, the composer Emmanuel Chabrier is sitting in a theatre box.

EDGAR DEGAS
The Dance Class, circa 1873-1876
Oil on canvas, 85 × 75 cm
Bequest of Count Isaac Camondo, 1911

→ In front of a group of ballerinas stands the small yet imposing silhouette of Jules Perrot the ballet master. Degas did not only spend time watching the Opera from his seat, he also visited backstage where he would sketch the dancers warming up or resting.

PAINTING

AUGUSTE RENOIR
Dance in the City, 1882-1883
Oil on canvas, 180 × 90 cm
Acquisition by "dation", 1978

AUGUSTE RENOIR
Dance in the Country, 1882-1883
Oil on canvas, 180 × 90 cm
Acquisition by "dation", 1979

→ Renoir painted the two pieces as a pair to compare a leisurely moment in the pleasant country environment of Bougival –the model here is Aline Charigot Renoir's sweetheart– with a more formal and elegant social event.

AUGUSTE RENOIR
The Swing, 1876
Oil on canvas, 92 × 73 cm
Bequest of Gustave Caillebotte, 1894

→ In 1875 Renoir was making
enough money to rent extra
space Rue Cortot near
Montmartre. In the back garden,
which according to the artist
looked like "an abandoned park",
he painted *The Swing*, praised
by Zola for the "golden dust"
and "gentle rays of light"
that illuminate the painting.

AUGUSTE RENOIR
Torso, Sun Effect, circa 1875-1776
Oil on canvas, 81 × 65 cm
Bequest of Gustave Caillebotte, 1894

→ Amongst the Impressionists,
Renoir consistently spent the
most time working on nudes.
His favorite type was a female
model with a sweet face, a small
chin and most of all, as shown
in this piece, a voluptuous body
that took the light well, similar
to the women chosen by Rubens.

AUGUSTE RENOIR
*Dance at Le Moulin
de la Galette*, **1876**
Oil on canvas, 131 × 175 cm
Bequest by Gustave Caillebotte,
1894

→ Renoir asked several
of his friends –as witnessed
by the critic Georges
Rivière– to pose for him
so that he could paint on
the motif the wonders
of changing light. *Le
Moulin de la Galette* was
a "café-concert" (café
where singers entertain the
customers) in Montmartre
that was set between
two windmills, the *Blute-
Fin* and the *Radet*. In the
background people are
dancing under the light
globes swinging from
the latticework above;
in the foreground, a woman
and her daughter sitting
on a bench are involved
in an animated
conversation with a man
whose back is all the viewer
can see. Two other persons
are also sitting at their
table; they are smoking
and drinking a refreshment.
The painting is filled with
details: the acacia leaves,
the ruffles enhancing
the clothes, fleeting
expressions...
By depicting the crowded
and lively "guinguettes",
Renoir recorded for
posterity, as eulogised
by Rivière, "a particular
moment of Parisian
lifestyle", signing an
important Impressionist
manifesto with his painting
travelled by a joyous
energy.

A Modern art

Cézanne (1839-1906) had a strong personality and despite his brutish appearance was extremely intelligent; he lived as a recluse refusing any form of compromise. A great admirer of tradition –he venerated Rubens, Puget, Chardin and the like– he nevertheless loathed academic epigones and was constantly rejected by the official instances. Because of the aesthetic orientations he took after meeting Pissarro in the early 1870s –fragmenting the brushstroke– and his noted presence at the 1874 exhibition with his much appreciated *House of the Hanged Man*, he was labelled an Impressionist. Still, he did not in fact belong to any group in particular; he persistently pursued his own convictions endeavouring to depict his "perceptions" using energetic brushstrokes to produce his unique compositions. His contemporaries never really understood the greatness of his vision: the elaborate balance ruling Cézanne's compositions takes each element into account leaving no peripheral or secondary areas unattended. Even though he worshipped nature his paintings were structured as distinctive architectural pieces. "Maybe I am just the primitive artist of a new art" he commented. He was also a perfectly mature classical artist.

PAUL CÉZANNE
Apples and Oranges, circa 1899
Oil on canvas, 74 × 93 cm
Bequest of Count Isaac de Camondo, 1911

→ Cézanne (1839-1906), who once declared he wished "Impressionism would become as solid and lasting as museum art", constructs his still-lives as if he were practicing a complex and daring enterprise in which the props –fruit, crockery, table cloth etc.– are all pieces of a unique architectural object.

PAUL CÉZANNE
Sainte-Victoire Mountain, circa 1890
Oil on canvas, 65 × 95.2 cm
Donation of the grand-daughter of Auguste Pellerin under usufruct, 1969

→ There are over eighty versions of Cézanne's *Sainte-Victoire*. When this mountain, which towers over his birthplace of Provence, was touched by the unique Mediterranean light it stirred the artist's soul, and awakened his sense of "perception". Here the landscape seems to surge towards the viewer and the colors are as if moved by a convex thrust.

PAUL CÉZANNE
Woman with Coffee Pot, circa 1890-1895
Oil on canvas, 130 × 97 cm
Gift of M. and Mrs. Jean Victor Pellerin, 1956

→ This woman was probably a strict and unyielding maid who worked for the artist at his home of Jas de Bouffan. Her strong presence and build are the result of a simple geometric construct. "Nature must be transcribed by using the cylinder, the sphere and the cone" advised Cézanne.

In order to understand the itinerary of Claude Monet (1840-1926), it is important to remember the long period of rejection he endured as a consequence of his ambitious aesthetic choices. From the 1880s and even more so in the 1890s, Monet's tender, bright, euphoric Impressionism evolved to become complex and even radical. He began using the surface of the canvas to record the passing of time, as shown in his series of haystacks and cathedrals in which he captured the ebb and flow of light and perception. By 1900, when he had finally acquired recognition, visitors from round the world hoped to meet the artist at his home since 1883, in Giverny. But he was not a socialite and preferred the company of his family and friends –namely Senator Georges Clemenceau a close and essential friend until the end– and his water-lilies. He planted the flowers himself in the water-garden he designed from scratch. He dedicated no less than two hundred decorative panels to his water-lilies, produced over thirty years during times of intense sadness –mourning, war, doubt, cataracts...– but serving a breathtaking "cosmic vision", as phrased by André Masson.

CLAUDE MONET
Blue Water-lilies, circa 1916-1919
Oil on canvas, 204 × 200 cm
Acquisition, 1981

→ Monet's inspiration and what he called "his most beautiful masterpiece" was quite simply his water-garden at Giverny. He began painting his water-lilies series in 1897. During the First World War his production increased significantly; close-up frames void of horizon and steeped in colors, they were works of peace, harmony and beauty and, in his own words, "the only way he could take part in the victory".

CLAUDE MONET
Haystacks, end of summer, 1891
Oil on canvas, 60.5 × 100.8 cm
Acquisition, 1975

→ Commenting on the *Haystacks*, Octave Moreau wrote: "One can sense, as if one were looking at someone's face, the changing emotions, the underlying passions, the moral dilemmas, the surges of internal joy, the melancholy, the pain, all those feelings that churn within." Thus a series of apparently unimportant landscapes of Vexin marked an historical turning point for modern painting. Kandinsky, the painter of abstraction, recalls a sort of epiphany when he saw Monet's work.

CLAUDE MONET
Rouen Cathedral series, 1892-1894
The Tour Saint-Romain Portal, Morning Effect, 1893
The Portal, Morning Sun, 1893
The Portal, Grey Weather, 1892
The Portal and the Tour Saint-Romain, 1893-1894
Oil on canvas, 106.5 cm × 73.2 cm; 92.2 × 63 cm; 100.2 × 65.4 cm; 107 × 73.5 cm
Bequest of Count Isaac de Camondo, 1911

→ "Everything changes, even stone" declared Monet when speaking of his "nightmarish" project, as he also named it. In February 1892 he began working on a series depicting the Rouen cathedral altered by passing time and changing light. Twenty eight versions are known to this day. It is a "moment about man himself", commented Georges Clemenceau, in 1895, when he was trying to convince the French President to come and admire Monet's sublime pictorial display.

Neo-impressionism

Although Neo-impressionism was a product of the same principles as those put forth by Monet and his companions, it brought to the concept of division of colours an entirely new perspective. Going beyond the intuitive approach, neo-impressionist aesthetics were based on the rigorous scientific premises promoted by Eugène Chevreul and Charles Henry. Their incredibly ambitious objective, as defined by Signac, was to "obtain the greatest amount of luminosity, coloration and harmony as possible", reaching a level "that would seem impossible to obtain with any other media". In order to achieve this, the "neos" used touches of pure apposed colours which set each other off, in accordance with the rule of simultaneous contrasting; an optical effect which causes colours to mix in the eye of the viewer, exempting the artist from doing so himself. In 1886, during the eighth Impressionist exhibition on the second floor of the Maison Dorée, the movement was noted for the controversy caused by Seurat's piece *The Grand Jatte*, in which the "figures looked like cardboard cut-outs" according to artist Alfred Stevens. For a while, Camille Pissarro and his son Lucien adhered to the new formal approach championed by the younger generation; which also voiced their political inclinations toward libertarian and anarchist ideas. Seurat was convinced that mastering art was a form of "hygiene" for the eye and the mind, and as such painting should be committed, because of its impact on the nervous system, to improving society and bringing about Paradise on earth. Despite the apparent domination of colour, the works of Signac, and even more so those of Seurat, are characterized by extraordinarily clean lines; indeed without being drawn per se, they are simply defined by coloured dots ("points" in French). Thus, the derogatory term of "pointillism" used at the time.

PAUL SIGNAC
Women at the Well, also called *Young Women from Provence at the Well* (decoration for a panel in half-light), **1892**
Oil on canvas, 195 × 131 cm
Acquisition, 1979

→ Beyond its anecdotic aspect typical of genre scenes, this painting, made up of an accumulation of radiant colours, implements the political point of view upheld by Signac (1863-1935) and the neo-impressionists: painting must sublimate harmony and happiness in order to encourage their realisation.

HENRI EDMOND CROSS
The Golden Isles (Hyères Island), **1891-1892**
Oil on canvas, 59 × 54 cm
Acquisition from the Fénéon sale, 1947

→ With Seurat and Signac, Cross (1856-1910) was the third leader of the neo-impressionist movement. This landscape is composed of three strips –sand, sea and sky –; it depicts the Hyères islands in the Mediterranean, the scene is fragmented into small round touches. The result is as intangible as music.

GEORGES SEURAT
The Circus, **1891**
Oil on canvas, 185 × 152 cm
Bequest of John Quinn, 1924

→ Located in Pigalle, Paris, the Fernando Circus was magnificent, it boasted a 21 meter high cast iron ceiling and seating for two thousand. On the ring a circus rider and a number of other figures seem to be floating in mid-air. The divisionism of Seurat's (1859-1891) light coloured touches makes for fluid, flexible outlines.

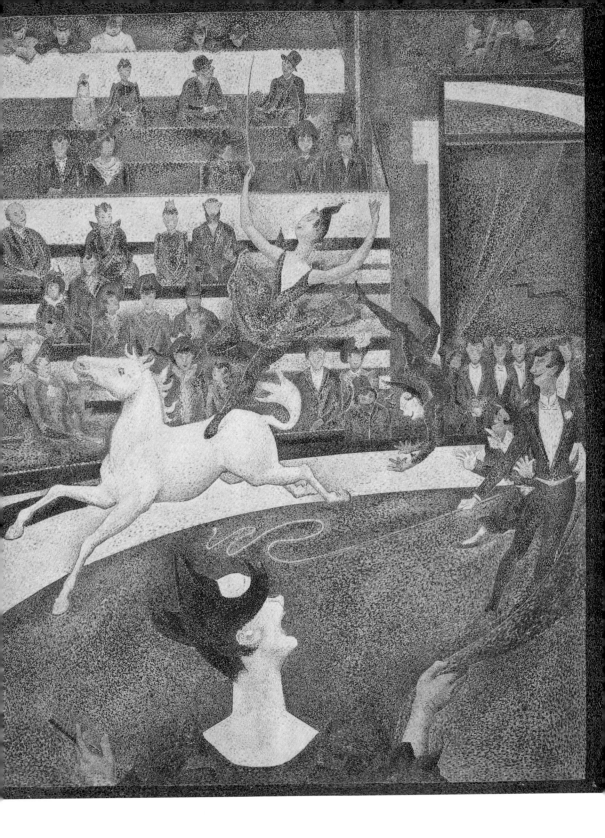

Post-impressionism

The term of Post-impressionism is more «convenient than accurate», observed the art historian John Rewald. It designates the artistic production of a variety of painters that were hostile towards academism, namely Gauguin, Van Gogh and Toulouse-Lautrec, and who had benefitted from the revolutionary aesthetics of Monet and Renoir. The forefathers and successors both have in common a bold colour palette, expressive drawing, the power to suggest rather than describe, and the use of contemporary subjects. Lautrec, in the wake of Manet and Degas, depicts Parisian life in Montmartre: its brothels, cabarets, and famous actresses. Still, Post-impressionism also contributed significant evolutions of its own such as the prominent place given to subjectivity and interiority. In Van Gogh's work the choice of colours and the energy in the brushstrokes expressed painful and violent torment, even a form of madness. Subject to terrible psychotic fits, in fact, the artist was sent to the Saint-Rémy-de-Provence asylum

after he mutilated himself in 1888. Meanwhile Gauguin and his young follower Émile Bernard, both developed in Pont-Aven a style that was just as avant-guard but more level-headed and reasonable, based on a homogenous design and style named "Synthetism".

Van Gogh, who committed suicide in 1890, and Gauguin who exiled to an island in the southern hemisphere where he died, shared a short, tense, period (1887-1888) of friendship. They both suffered from lack of recognition –the Dutch painter only sold one piece during his lifetime –, and were both labeled as "accursed artists", for despite their incredible genius and valuable impact they were never recognized during their lifetime. Their Post-impressionist approach gave birth to new modernist movements in the twentieth century: fiery fauvism, tormented expressionism, and the solar fervour of Matisse as well as Picasso's reinvention of beauty.

PAUL GAUGUIN
Vairumati, **1897**
Oil on canvas, 73.5 × 92.5 cm
Became part of the Louvre collection as a clause of the peace treaty with Japan in 1959

→ In Tahiti, where Gauguin (1848-1903) left to live freely, away from economic and moral constraints, he often paid homage to young women in hieratic and colourful compositions that show them occupied at their daily tasks. Vairumati is a character from local folk legends.

PAUL GAUGUIN
The White Horse, **1898**
Oil on canvas, 140,5 × 92 cm
Acquisition, 1927

→ The lines drawn by the boughs of the *bouroas* (local tree), the water and the animals all compose a tableau of sensual and harmonious curves. This large format executed by Gauguin in the latter part of his career, belongs to a group of paintings about the relationship between man and horse, the animal had been imported to Polynesia by the Spanish in the Sixteenth century.

PAINTING

VINCENT VAN GOGH
Van Gogh's room in Arles,
1889
Oil on canvas, 57.3 × 73.5 cm
Became part of the Louvre
collection as a clause of the
peace treaty with Japan in 1959

→ There are several
versions of Vincent
Van Gogh's (1853-1890)
room in Arles. It was
a favorite subject
of his: the combination
of colours and the simple
environment express what
he called "absolute rest".

VINCENT VAN GOGH
*The Church at Auvers-sur-
Oise, view of the chevet*,
1890
Oil on canvas, 93 × 74.5 cm
Acquisition with the aid of
Paul Gachet and an anonymous
Canadian donation, 1951

→ Vincent Van Gogh,
Van Gogh painted
this piece at the very
end of his life just
before his suicide.
The picturesque simplicity
of the church chevet
and the lone passer-by
is transcended by the frank
colours, the energetic
brushstroke and the slight
feeling of instability the
wavy motif produces.

VINCENT VAN GOGH
Portait of the Artist, **1889**
Oil on canvas, 65 × 54.2 cm
Gift of Paul and Marguerite
Gachet, 1949

→ Vincent Van Gogh,
Like Rembrandt,
his most important
role model, Van Gogh
produced many self-
portraits painted at
different times of his
life. They recorded the
evolution of his physical
and moral state. Here,
the withered face
contrasts with the hard
piercing eyes and the
undulating background.

VINCENT VAN GOGH
Starry Night, 1888
Oil on canvas, 73.5 × 92 cm
Donation under usufruct
of M. and Mrs. Robert Khan-
Sriber in memory of M. and Mrs
Fernand Moch, 1975

→ From his arrival in
Paris in 1886 and until his
suicide in 1890, Vincent
Van Gogh experienced
periods of intense
creativity –painting up to
several pieces a day– and
bouts of deep and painful
depression. In Arles he
was amazed by the clear
light of the south: "I am
absolutely convinced
that nature as it is here is
what is needed to work
with colour", he declared.
Paradoxically, one of his
obsessions was to find
a way to capture this
radiance in a night view, as
he had confided to Émile
Bernard: "I wonder when
I shall do that *Starry Sky*,
the painting that forever
has been on my mind".
From the left bank of the
Rhone River, he painted
the city from above, lit up
with gas lighting. He filled
the sky artificially with the
southern star formation
of the Big Dipper –which
was in fact behind him.
In the foreground the
diminutive figures of a
couple. The contrasts
between the deep blues
and the bright yellows,
structured by energetic
brushstrokes and a
spacious composition,
all combine to make this
work one of the most
remarkable landscapes
of the 19th century,
and one of Van Gogh's
favourites as well.

**HENRI DE
TOULOUSE-LAUTREC**
Jane Avril dancing, **circa 1892**
Oil on canvas, 85.5 × 45 cm
Bequest of Antonin Personnaz, 1937

→ With large brushstrokes
that do not entirely cover
the canvas, this piece
by Toulouse-Lautrec
(1864-1901) pays homage
to the extraordinary energy
and scenic qualities of his
friend Jane Avril when she
is dancing a French Cancan.
He contributed to her fame
by further illustrating her
on two renowned posters,
notably the one for the *Divan
Japonais.*

**HENRI DE TOULOUSE-
LAUTREC**
The Clown Cha-U-Kao, **1895**
Oil on canvas, 58 × 43 cm
Bequest of Count Isaac
de Camondo, 1911

→ Lautrec particularly liked
to capture women during
intimate moments, notably
the stars of cabaret shows.
On a simple piece
of cardboard he produced
the portrait of the female
clown whose fake Japanese
name was Cha-U-Kao
–a play on the word *chahut*,
the name of a group grand
finale dance. Here he used
the circular shape of the large
yellow collar of her costume
to bring movement to
the composition.

The Nabis

PAINTING

In 1890 the Nabis group –nabi meaning prophet in Hebrew– consisted of a number of young artists born around 1870: Denis, Vuillard, Bonnard, Sérusier as well as Ranson, Ibels, Roussel, Verkade, Maillol and Valloton. They were very cultured, for the most part involved in occultism, and developed a particular type of aesthetic premise bathed in a strange, mysterious atmosphere. The members would meet at 25 Boulevard Montparnasse at Paul Ranson's; their encounters followed a hallucinating ritual by which the enthroned were welcomed as new brothers under Jehovah's direction. Their subjects were drawn from every day and private life but were rendered in a surprisingly bold fashion. Their notion of space is rid of the illusion of perspective, depth and relief; they prefer a plane, off-centered, elliptic and pure form. All of which were inspired by Japanese prints and symbolism – especially Redon's work – and a "master class" taught by Gauguin. In October 1888, Sérusier and Gauguin were sitting on the river bank at Pont-Aven when the now famous conversation took place – the resulting painting was called *Talisman*. The master was supporting a subjective approach to the landscape by which the mind's eye should translate what one actually saw. "How do you see these trees? Asked Gauguin; they are yellow. Well then, use yellow; and that shadow? Sort of bluish; paint in pure ultramarine blue then; and those red leaves? Use vermillion." In the end the subject disappeared behind the composition thus becoming autonomous, almost abstract, made of shapes and colours. A process that brings to mind Maurice Denis's founding definition: "One must remember that a painting – before being a battle horse, or a nude woman, or a description of any kind – is first and foremost a flat surface on which colours are spread and assembled with order." The group only lasted and exhibited together for a short time; however its members all enjoyed remarkable careers and most of them continued seeing each other frequently during the twentieth century.

PIERRE BONNARD
Dusk, also called *A Round of Croquet*, 1892
Oil on canvas, 130.5 × 162.2 cm
Gift of Daniel Wildenstein through the "Société des amis du musée d'Orsay", 1985

→ Croquet was fashionable in England at the end of the 1850s. Here a leisurely family moment is transformed with amazing skill into a series of decorative motifs. Maurice Denis complemented his friend Bonnard (1867-1947) for the plane effect and declared: "M. Bonnard has a very personal way of interpreting Japanese prints".

FÉLIX VALLOTTON
The Ball, also called
*A Corner of the Park
with a Child*, 1899
Oil on cardboard glued to wood,
49.2 × 62 cm
Bequest of Carle Dreyfus, 1953

→ A child is depicted
as he races to catch
a red ball. In his painting
Vallotton (1865-1925)
opposes the sandy
ground, seen from a low
angle, to the expanse
of green lawn at the top
of which stand two tiny
silhouettes. The curving
axis of the composition
intensifies the feeling
of distance between
the figures.

MAURICE DENIS
The Muses, 1893
Oil on canvas, 171 × 137.5 cm
Acquisition, 1932

→ What could have simply
been a group of women in
a park has been transformed
by Maurice Denis (1870-1943)
into a solemn and sacred vision.
The forest is stylized to such
an extent that it appears
to be a ritual environment
where the characters are not
just communicating with nature
but connected to the mystery
of enlightenment.

ÉDOUARD VUILLARD
*Panels designed for Alexander
Natanson's Dining Room,
or Public Gardens: Girls Playing
and The Question,* 1894
Oil on canvas,
214.5 × 88 cm, 214.5 × 92 cm
Bequest of Mrs. Alexander Radot, 1978
*Public Gardens: The Nannies,
The Conversation and The Red
Parasol,* 1894
Tempera on canvas, 213.8 × 154 cm,
213.5 × 154 cm, 214 × 81 cm
Acquisition, 2009

→ Vuillard (1868-1940) was inspired by the Tuileries gardens
–he lived nearby– and the Bois de Boulogne next to the
mansion of Alexandre Natanson who had commissioned
these decorative panels.
The scenes are evocative rather than descriptive, leaving
the imagination free to discover scenes of everyday life:
walking, games, conversations etc. Nannies watching
over children are a recurring motif among the Nabis, still
Vuillard has also included classical references such as the
Cluny tapestries, and the French 18th century atmosphere
–Fragonard and Watteau– and of course, Japanese prints.
The Public Gardens are a magnificent and technically
difficult piece to realize –using tempera rather than oil
paint– Alexander Natanson and his family were enchanted.
The nine mural panels were installed in the ground floor
dining room of their mansion, and inaugurated
in February 1895 during a splendid reception
where three hundred peopled applauded the piece.

Symbolism and Expressionism

In the second half of the 19th century there were two trends within the artistic avant-garde: the first intended to capture what they saw with as much sincerity and accuracy as possible –Realism, Naturalism, Impressionism etc.– the second sought to translate the invisible and intangible into their work; this was the case of the Symbolists. It started with an important literary movement led, in France, by Baudelaire, and continued by Mallarmé, Verlaine and Huysmans. As for the visual arts Symbolism was exemplified by the works of Gustave Moreau, Pierre Puvis de Chavannes and Odilon Redon. Although those three artists had distinctive styles they shared a strong taste for the imaginary and dreams, choosing allegoric, mysterious and even fantastic subjects – Gustave Moreau's flora, and Odilon Redon's hybrid beings, for instance. Contrary to the representation of nature, landscapes and outdoors painting, as preferred by the first group, Symbolists practiced their art in the studio and chose complex, sometimes even almost hermetic, intellectual themes. In order to develop their personal visions fully they all had their own particular style: extremely hieratic in Puvis de Chavanne's case, and effects of a grey palette in that of Eugène Carrière, for example. As for Expressionism –the term did not emerge until 1910, in Germany– the idea was to intensify the psychological perception of life by extolling and dramatizing it. Van Gogh and Gauguin did show some signs of nascent Expressionism, however the true pioneers came from Central and Northern Europe: Edvard Munch, James Ensor, and Gustavo Klimt etc. Emotions, whether joyful or tormented, memories and fantasies were clearly included into the interpretation of the subject, which even became, at times, only a pretext through which feelings could be transmitted. At a period when psychoanalysis was gaining recognition the advent of this specific form of aesthetics was far from surprising.

GUSTAVE MOREAU
Orpheus, 1865
Oil on wood, 154 × 99.5 cm
Acquisition, 1866

→ Gustave Moreau (1826-1898) had a penchant for myths; here he has represented one of the great figures of poetry and creativity, Orpheus. The unfortunate lover of Eurydice was killed by the Maenads, upset by the hero's rejection of their love. One of them is crying over a lyre in which is embedded Orpheus's face.

ODILON REDON
Closed Eyes, 1890
Oil on canvas, 44 × 36 cm
Acquisition, 1904

→ This evanescent, neither quite male nor quite female face seems to be in a sensual and mystical trance. The closed eyes are a typically symbolist invitation to dream and meditate. Redon (1840-1916) undoubtedly transformed his wife Camille into some sort of deity.

PIERRE PUVIS DE CHAVANNES
Young Girls by the Sea, 1879
Oil on canvas,
205.4 × 156 cm
Gift of Robert Gérard, 1970

→ The impeccably pure lines and melancholic atmosphere rendered by the matte greys and blues set Puvis de Chavannes's (1824-1898) paintings out of time and space. The young girls in solid colours are represented according to traditional standards of beauty; his style was much appreciated for its highly decorative quality.

FERNAND KHNOPFF
Incense, **1898**
Oil on canvas, 86 × 50 cm
Acquisition, 2007

→ *Incense* is an allegory referring
to one of the three Wise Men's
gifts. However the true subject
is elsewhere. The colour palette,
limited to a variation of greys and
browns, used here by Fernand
Khnopff (1858-1921) make for
a splendid rendering of his sister
Marguerite, for whom he had
a passionate admiration.
Her dress, embroidered with
a motif of large thistles, adds
mystery to her beauty.

EDWARD BURNE-JONES
The Wheel of Fortune, **1875-1883**
Oil on canvas, 200 × 100 cm
Acquisition, 1980

→ Influenced by the return
of the aesthetics of Botticelli
and Michel-Angelo, Burne-Jones
(1833-1898) was a great master
of traditional allegories of
life, from birth to death, he
represented all the good and
bad fortunes of destiny. To the
right, a slave, a king and a poet
are caught in the gigantic wheel
driven pitilessly by the goddess,
standing on the left.

PAINTING

EDVARD MUNCH
Summer Night at
Aasgaardstrand, 1904
Oil on canvas, 99 × 103.5 cm
Acquisition, 1986

→ Originally from Norway,
Munch (1863-1944) was
traumatized by a terrible
childhood. Though
he is a descendant
of Impressionism, his
landscapes are much
more tormented and
exalted, and reflect his
fragile psyche; he suffered
several breakdowns.

GUSTAV KLIMT
Rosebushes under Trees, circa 1905
Oil on canvas, 110.2 × 110.2 cm
Acquisition, 1980

→ Klimt (1862-1918) spent
his whole career battling to
abolish the barrier between fine
arts and decorative arts. Here
the square canvas is filled with
a massive amount of dabs
of colour, similar to the Neo-
impressionist technique.
The sheer quantity of leaves
and roses erases any illusion
of relief, creating a plane space
resembling a mosaic.

HENRI ROUSSEAU, ALIAS LE DOUANIER ROUSSEAU
The Snake Charmer, 1907
Oil on canvas, 167 × 189.5 cm
Bequest of Jacques Doucet, 1936

→ The mysterious atmosphere that emanates from this painting by Douanier Rousseau
(1844-1910), derives from a combination of primitivism, exoticism and a form of childish naivety.
The precise and beautifully painted representation of the jungle –observed at the Natural History
Museum in Paris– makes for an enchanting and slightly unsettling background for the wild looking,
black version of Eve.

PHOTOGRAPHY

Photography appeared in 1839, when Daguerre officially demonstrated his process at the Paris Académie des Sciences. The taste for
photography began expanding immediately, the technique was conti-
nuously improved and started impacting business, science, art and leisure. Suddenly this new visual object was being produced and used
everywhere. As Orsay was the first Fine Arts museum to build a photography collection from scratch, the purchase policies could be fine-
tuned with regard to the considerable production already available.

The curators designing the department were intent on showing the
evolution of the technology, and illustrating the various stages with
high quality documents and as many original photographs –whether
negatives or prints– as possible; as indeed, only documents produced
by their original authors reveal the artists' touch and can therefore
contribute with the most significance to understanding the medium
and its history. However, it also seemed appropriate to acquire, besides
masterpieces, less prestigious proofs and series that would be useful to
show the production issues encountered in the past. It seemed important to investigate the relationship between photography and other
existing arts while bearing in mind the international standing of Orsay
museum. Lastly, rather than collecting similar pieces to those of existing French public institutions the museum chose to complete them
with different works.

With all these criteria in mind the first pieces were bought in public auc-
tions as well as from private collectors; calls for donations were issued,
mostly towards photographers' descendants that had kept their ancestor's stocks; and requests made to institutions that owned photographic records.

Thus sixteen thousand pieces were acquired between 1979, when the
first purchases began, and 1986, when the museum opened; a figure
that has increased to almost fifty thousand since.   Joëlle Bolloch

A daguerreotype is a very special device, the equipment required to produce a direct positive is cumbersome and complicated, also, in the early years, each picture had to be shot individually and exposure time could take as long as several minutes. However, the technique soon became widespread and, in the 1850s, it was being used by mostly professional photographers and a few amateur enthusiasts. The Orsay daguerreotype collection was greatly enhanced by the significant Kodak Pathé donation that was received in 1983. When William Henry Fox Talbot from Britain, invented a method by which several proofs could be produced from a single shot, his process gradually replaced that of Louis Daguerre. The Museum owns a marvellous collection of works by those who are called the French "primitives", namely Gustave Le Gray, Édouard Baldus, Henri Le Secq, Charles Nègre etc. Paper negatives were little by little replaced by glass plates coated with collodion, while albumen paper was preferred over salt-paper positives.

Then, circa 1880, exposure time and the size of the equipment required were reduced thanks to the use of glass plates coated with silver-bromide gelatin. The arrival of celluloid negatives was another turning point as it enabled Kodak to begin distributing the first commercial cameras. The various photomechanical processes are all represented in the collection from Charles Nègre's helioengravings to the fifty issues of Alfred Stieglitz's review *Camera Work*, including photolithographs from Auguste Salzmann's calotypes (sometimes called Talbotypes) taken during his trip to the Holy Land. The collections cover the eight decades since the invention of the art, and display examples of a broad variety of techniques such as the first attempts at colour: autochromes, and other marginal processes such as cyanotypes, research with color pigments, and the use of gum dichromate by pictorialists, as well as collage and photomontage.

LOUIS ADOLPHE HUMBERT DE MOLARD
Louis Dodier as a Prisoner,
1847
Daguerreotype, 11.5 × 15.5 cm
Gift of the Braunschweig family, 1988

→ Hubert de Molard (1800-1874) was a wealthy amateur and daguerreotype enthusiast. When he had Louis Dodier, his steward, pose for the picture he was not exactly planning a portrait but the sort of staged tableau that was so fashionable at that time.

PAUL HAVILAND
Florence Peterson in a Kimono
with a bouquet, circa 1909
Cyanotype, 25.4 × 20.3 cm
Acquisition, 1993

→ The specific hues
of cyanotypes is induced
by the use of ferricyanide salt
which, when exposed to light
turned to Prussian blue.
The process discovered
by Sir John Herschel by 1842,
was used by photographers
and architects to produce what
was commonly called "blueprints".
The colour corresponds to Paul
Haviland's (1880-1950) symbolist
period.

HEINRICH KÜHN
Drum and Tin Soldier, 1910
Autochrome Lumière, 18 × 24 cm
Acquisition, 2008

→ Heinrich Kühn (1866-1944),
whose personal motto was "Praise
the sun, praise the light", was an
Austrian Pictorialist; he is known
for the pictures of his children as
well as landscapes and still-lives,
and, from 1907, his autochromes.
The additive color "mosaic screen
plate" process is a technique
invented by the Lumière brothers
in 1904, it uses as a filter a glass
plate coated with grains of potato
starch coloured in blue, red and
green, and was the first colour
process to be commercialized.
It was generally used for
projection so it can be seen
as the ancestor of the slide.

Portraits, landscapes, and history... Atget, Cameron, Le Gray, Nadar

PHOTOGRAPHY

Before the invention of photography, portraits were painted or sculpted, therefore only accessible to the elites; the relatively low cost, the fact that it was a much faster process and reproduced the model with complete accuracy, made daguerreotypes affordable thus portraits were no longer a privilege of the elite; middle class people everywhere were having their image captured onto a metal plate. Orsay has a variety of splendid daguerreotype portraits, some of which were produced by the Americans Southworth and Hawes. Intellectuals and artists of the 1850s visited the studio of the Parisian photographer Félix Nadar, who was not content with simply capturing his models' physical resemblance and sought to reveal their "moral intelligence". The Museum also owns some outstanding portraits by the British photographers Julia Margaret Cameron and Lewis Carroll, as well as works by the Pictorialists Edward Steichen and Paul strand. Also, in 1995, Orsay purchased some twenty photo albums of a more anecdotique nature; they consist of calling card sized photographs by Eugène

Disdéri, which recorded life under the Second Empire. Copying nature has always been one of the main objectives of photography, as prove the many landscapes produced by the French "primitives" mentioned above, and those of the travelling photographers that gathered views from around the world, including the photographic records of the virgin territories of the Great American West, commissioned by the government.

Edifices, monuments, paintings, sculptures have been systematically photographed; all those pictures make for a virtual museum in which artists may find material to study while others might simply be happy to view places they cannot visit in person.

Meanwhile photography has also become an accessory to history, as it is a means of recording historical events – wars, conflicts, official visits –, and current events such as floods etc. Then, there are photographs of still-lives, artists' models, living tableaus... and the list could go on!

JULIA MARGARET CAMERON
Mrs Herbert Duckworth, also called *Julia Jackson, Mother of Virginia Woolf*, 1872
Carbon print, 39.8 × 25.5 cm
Gift of the Texbraun Gallery, 1986

➔ Julia Margaret Cameron (1815-1879) came from the Victorian establishment. She was not a professional photographer however she produced a number of portraits for the writers, poets, musicians and scientists that had become her friends. The close-up shots of her models' faces are vibrant with life.

FÉLIX NADAR
Charles Baudelaire Sitting in Nadar's Studio, circa 1855
Salt paper print, 21.2 × 16.5 cm
Acquisition thanks to the Patrimonial Fund, 1991

➔ Although Charles Baudelaire had often voiced his reservations concerning photography, he nevertheless had several portraits made by Félix Nadar (1820-1910). Previously a satirical cartoonist, Nadar's portraits show his keen sense of observation, as he manages to capture some of the most intimate aspects of his models' psychology.

GUSTAVE LE GRAY
Mediterranean Sea, Mont Agde, circa 1856
Albumen print from two negatives on damp collodion coated glass plates, 32.6 × 42 cm
Acquisition, 1990

→ Trained to become a painter, the legacy of Gustave Le Gray (1820-1884) consists of powerful pictures in which he privileged textures over detail. In his seascapes there are no picturesque scenes or ships battling against raging seas, his only subject is the reflection of clouds and sunlight on the water.

EUGÈNE ATGET
Parcheminerie Street, march 1913,
1913-1927
Albumen print from a negative
on silver-bromide gelatin coated
glass plates, 18.3 × 22.3 cm
Deposited by the French National Library,
1986

→ Eugène Atget (1857-1927)
accumulated over four thousand
shots of old Paris between 1897
and 1927: streets undergoing works,
shops about to be destroyed etc.
Commissioned by libraries and
museums, his photographs are
more than just records as his work
drew the attention of the surrealists
at the time.

Aesthetics and Pictorialism

Most photographers were acquainted with and belonged to the artistic circles of their times therefore, when they were not working on a strictly commercial order, they began taking liberties with the representation of reality. In fact, the difference between a fair and an exceptional daguerreotype was clearly due to the author's point of view on the subject. The negative positive techniques offered plenty of room for authorial choices in framing, lighting, exposure time, chemicals, plates... For instance, to produce his seascapes Gustave Le Gray used two negatives, one for the sea that was subjected to a longer exposure, the other for the sky; thus avoiding the overexposure of the latter which would be detrimental to the contrast effect. He would then cut the negatives in two and sea and sky were carefully assembled for the positive print.

Several decades later, Bonnard, and quite a few of his Nabi friends, realised the many advantages offered by the user-friendly Kodak camera. He began capturing scenes from his life, and more specifically with his companion Martha, with the same freedom of composition as in his paintings.

Up until World War I, Pictorialism appeared to be the only existing photography movement. It began in Great Britain on the premise that the operator's eye and sensitivity should rule over the subject matter. The trend began to spread to France, Austria and of course the United States with Alfred Stieglitz and Edward Steichen, both renowned proponents of the movement. The proofs are hand altered and gum dichromate or coloured pigments were sometimes added to obtain a variety of nuances on the print. In addition to contributing their original prints, Pictorialists also helped improve photomechanical techniques, notably through the commercialisation of the review *Camera Work*, published from 1903 to 1917.

ALFRED STIEGLITZ
The Steerage (1907), **1911**
Photomechanical print, 19.6 × 15.7 cm
Gift of the Georgia O'Keeffe Foundation,
2003

➔ The composition of this photograph is outstanding. The passengers –possibly immigrants on their way to New York City– are grouped on either side of the gangway as if there was a barrier between them. The persons on the top level appear to be mostly men dressed in dark clothes while the occupants of the lower level are women and children clad in light clothing. The pale coloured boater, worn by the man leaning over the railing, echoes the black hat of the man in the forefront of the lower level.

PIERRE BONNARD
Marthe in the Tub, Vernouillet,
circa 1908-1912
Modern print from a negative of silver
bromide flexible film, 3.8 × 5.5 cm
Donation under usufruct of the Terrasse
Estate, 1992

→ The dimensions of flexible
negatives from Kodak cameras
were no larger than 3.8 × 5.5 cm.
They enabled Bonnard (1867-
1947) to capture the spontaneous
attitudes and movements of
his models –his companion
Marthe, his nephews and nieces–
confirming again that there
was no separation between
his personal life and his work.

EDWARD STEICHEN
In Memoriam, 1904
Dichromatic gum print, 47.5 × 36 cm
Acquisition by the Fonds du Patrimoine
with a contribution from the National
Photography Commission, 1999

→ Female nudes were a favorite
with Pictorialists; this print
is one of the most prestigious
acquired by Orsay, it entered the
collection in 1999. The symbolist
atmosphere in this photograph
by Steichen (1879-1973) is a result
of his skillful use of light and
shadows, their interplay revealing
or masking the various parts
of the body.

DECORATIVE ARTS

View of the Amont Pavilion room with a Nabi décor.

The diversity of the Orsay Museum decorative arts collections reflects that of the 1848-1914 production; indeed, the rich variety of creative expression of that period offers us significant insights into the development of current trends. Though no distinct style prevailed during the 19th century, it was certainly a prolific time during which the many original and distinctive works are indicative of a strong drive toward modernity and the desire to abolish any notion of hierarchy between the arts –notably but not exclusively– in England with the Arts and Crafts movement. The gradual introduction of decorativeness into the various Art Nouveau trends and the evolution towards the pure lines and formal precision of Scottish, German and Austrian households, are all preparing the advent of what will be called, in the twentieth century, Design. Thus, the historical significance of the Orsay collection of decorative arts lies in the works themselves and, in how they have inspired contemporary interior decoration.

A great deal of important pieces from various institutions such as the National Furniture Store, the Ministry of Foreign Affairs, the Louvre and the Cluny Museums were transferred to Orsay at its creation; and since then the collections have been regularly augmented. Also, thanks to the acquisition policy, implemented as soon as the museum was planned, the collections could be enhanced with a great deal of new purchases such as masterpieces from the World Fairs (Expositions Universelles) and examples of the rarely seen decorative production from foreign countries like Germany or the Scandinavian nations. Finally the department was enriched by generous patrons: the 2005 Rispal donation, for instance, brought in about two hundred and fifty art nouveau pieces.

Jérémie Cerman

Eclecticism

DECORATIVE ARTS

During the second half of the 19th century, the novel possibilities provided by industrial development generated a taste for mixed styles in ornamentation while launching a number of debates on subjects such as the interaction between art and industry, the concept of combining the beautiful and the useful. In this context, the artists involved in applied arts began promoting the study of great historical traditions, drawing their inspiration from them and, from then on, offering an array of reinterpretations. Consequently, from Neo-Gothic to Neo-Rococo, including Neo-Byzantine and Neo-Renaissance, the decorative arts production of 1850 to 1880 was ruled by historicist and eclectic trends. One of the emblematic realizations of eclecticism is the décor and architecture of the Opera House built by Charles Garnier (1825-1898), for which works began in 1860 and lasted fifteen years.

One of the most stunning luxury pieces –and a pure product of eclecticism– crafted at the time was *The Toilette*

of the Duchess of Parma; it was the result of a collaboration involving several major artistic personalities. Ordered in 1845, it was completed in 1851 and entered into the first World Fair in London that same year. As these international events were an opportunity for peaceful confrontation between nations, masterpieces from a variety of techniques were entered into the competition. This was the case for the Neo-Greek style table designed by the sculptor Émile Hébert (1828-1893) and manufactured by the Servant establishment; typical of Second Empire taste it was exhibited during the 1878 Exposition Universelle in Paris. Amongst the large ensembles of that period, one must note the Marquees of Païva's mansion and its Renaissance style interior decorations, for which many artists collaborated under the direction of the architect Pierre Manguin (1815-1869), including Albert Ernest Carrier-Belleuse (1824-1887) and Jules Dalou (1838-1902), who signed the reception room consoles.

ALBERT ERNEST CARRIER-BELLEUSE, JULES DALOU
Console for the Reception Room of the Hôtel de Païva, 1864-1865
Gilded (gold and silver) and patinated bronze, red marble, onyx and alabaster, 110 × 161 × 58 cm
"Dation", 1996

ÉMILE HÉBERT
Neo-Greek Style Table, 1878
Ebony and ebonized wood, gilded and patinated bronze, Saint-Jean "fleuri" marble, 80 × 109 × 72.5 cm
Acquisition, 2002

**JEAN FEUCHÈRE,
FRANÇOIS DÉSIRÉ
FROMENT-MEURICE
AND ADOLPHE VICTOR
GEOFFROY-DECHAUME**
*Duchess of Parma Table and Toilette
Ensemble*, 1845-1851
Niello incrust on silver gilt, engraved iron,
oak structure, and support structure of gold
and silver gilt, iron gilded copper, enameled
and silver gilded bronze and garnets,
80 × 188 × 109 cm (table).
130 × 92 × 50.4 cm (mirror)
Acquisition, 1981

DECORATIVE ARTS

During the second half of the 19th century, at a time when most of continental Europe was experimenting with past styles, Great-Britain was pioneering new directions in decorative arts. Partisans of Gothic Revival –namely Augustus Welby Nothmore Pugin (1812-1852), who contributed to the reconstruction and decorations of Westminster Palace– refused to use illusion and supported the return of a true gothic form. Following Pugin came those who founded the Design Reform Movement, at the 1851 World Fair in London, such as Owen Jones (1809-1874) author of the famous *Grammar of Ornament* (1856). Strongly against naturalist representation, and more specifically any rococo tendencies, Jones contends that vegetal forms should be rationalized and subjected to the rules of geometry.

William Morris (1834-1896), a decorator, poet and militant writer, is one of the leading figures of the revival of British decorative arts. Deploring the drab and ugly aesthetic choices proposed by industry, he vehemently denounced mechanisation for its disastrous impact on decorative arts.

In his opinion, only the return to craftsmanship and stylised shapes drawn from nature could revive decorative arts. As a follower of John Ruskin, who linked artistic creation to morality and liberty, Morris's ideals were rooted in social considerations; he believed that art should be created by the people for the people. To him improving everyday life had as much to do with household environment as with the social conditions of the working class.

Until the end of the century, the movement launched by Morris, generally listed under the heading of Arts and Crafts, included many contributors from Philip Webb (1831-1915) to Charles Voysey (1857-1941) and Walter Crane (1845-1915). Simultaneously, the Aesthetic Movement, strongly influenced by Japanese art, aspired to obtain pure aesthetic pleasure and opposed the utilitarian approach of Arts and Crafts; their inclination towards organic forms and curves announce the arrival of Art Nouveau and its world expansion.

**AUGUSTUS WELBY
NORTHMORE PUGIN**
*Door Panel from the New Westminster
Palace*, circa 1850
Sculpted oak and varnished oak, 67 × 62 cm
Acquisition, 1998

**WILLIAM FREND DE MORGAN,
WILLIAM MORRIS**
Wall Panelling, 1876-1877
Assembly of 66 enameled faience tiles
Gift of the "Société des Amis du musée d'Orsay", 1989

PHILIP WEBB
Sideboard, circa 1880
Dark varnished mahogany, partially painted and
gilded, painted and varnished embossed leather
Acquisition, 1979

Art Nouveau

DECORATIVE ARTS

Besides Great-Britain's role in the emergence of Art Nouveau, the movement drew from many other sources. In France for instance, and despite the rejection of historicist influences, some aspects of the works by Eugène Emmanuel Viollet-le Duc (1814-1879) influenced the 1900 style. The prevailing taste for Japanaserie, its artistic styles and vision of nature as well as the Japanese idea of living environments, also nourished the movement.

Hector Guimard (1867-1942) was one of the forerunners of Art Nouveau. With his Castel Béranger in Paris (1895-1898) he developed a style in which he banished the straight line and favoured curvilinear shapes. Guimard applied the famous "whiplash" lines, typical of Art Nouveau, to all decorative elements –furniture, stained-glass windows, wallpaper and wrought iron– in keeping with his idea of total art every single object of daily use had to blend in as it was considered as part of the artwork. In the 1900s, Paris was one of the main centres for Art Nouveau, as proved by the many initiatives launched at the time such as the "Art Nouveau Gallery" opened by Sigfried Bing (1838-1905) in late 1895, the flourish of works by Alphonse Mucha

(1860-1939), Georges Feure (1868-1943), and Eugène Grasset (1845-1917) as well as those of the designers belonging to "L'Art dans Tout" (art in everything). That period marked the artistic debut of many figures who, after the war, became leading representatives of Art Deco as were, for instance, Paul Follot (1877-1941) and Maurice Dufrène (1876-1955).

Several distinct regional centres began receiving international recognition, such as the town of Nancy (in Lorraine, a region in the north-east of France) where The Lorraine Industrial and Decorative Arts exhibition was held in 1894 at the Poirel Room, announcing the advent of a new cultural and artistic entity. The Art Nouveau style was particularly successful when applied to furniture, glassware and jewelry designed by artists such as René Lalique (1860-1945), Émile Gallé (1846-1904), Louis Majorelle (1859-1929) and the Daum establishment. Inlay and glass paste techniques, developed specifically in Nancy, were immediately compatible with a style that favored the effects of mixed materials.

ÉMILE GALLÉ
Still Waters, **1889-1890**
Several layers of blown crystal, matt base, surface layer
partly hammered, pieces of engraved glass, inclusions
of metal flecks (silver and mica), engraved cabochons set
with heat, engraved décor, 24 × 11 cm
"Dation", 1995

EUGÈNE GRASSET
Apparitions, **1900**
Brooch in chased gold; translucent
and opaque cloisonné enamel; ivory;
topaz cabochons, 3.9 × 6.2 × 1.3 cm
Acquisition, 1900

RENÉ LALIQUE
Brooch, **1899-1903**
Yellow and pink gold, translucent cloisonné
and open worked enamels, opaque
engraved enamel with three tourmalines,
8.2 × 2.8 × 4.6 cm
Gift of Miss Tarn (?) to the Luxembourg
Museum, 1907 or 1908

PAUL FOLLOT
*Double Bodied
Cabinet with Floral
Motif*, **circa 1912**
Gold painted wood, inlay
and sculpted elements,
165 × 188 × 65 cm
Acquisition, 2011

HECTOR GUIMARD
Smoke Room Seat, **1897**
Jarrah wood, chiselled metal,
modern seating,
260 × 262 × 66 cm
Acquisition, 1979

An International Movement

The international impact of the Art Nouveau movement had already been confirmed by the end of 1895 when Siegfried Bing opened his gallery in Paris. A collector and dealer of German origin, he showed a broad variety of Modern Style works from England, as well as pieces of distinctive craftsmanship by artists such as the Belgian Henry Van de Velde (1863-1957) and the American Louis Comfort Tiffany (1848-1933). Art Nouveau style pieces are found in households everywhere; even in Eastern Europe or Scandinavia as shown by the carpet designed by the Finnish painter Akseli Gallen-Kallela (1865-1931).

Besides Paris and Nancy, in Europe, Art Nouveau was pioneered simultaneously in Belgium, particularly in Brussels where Paul Hankar (1859-1901) and Victor Horta (1861-1947) were active. Also, when Henry Van de Velde abandoned painting in 1892, and began concentrating on decorative arts and the virtues of dynamic lines, he became one of the leading figures of the movement. In Liège, a more moderate formal approach was developed by Gustave Serrurier-Bovy (1858-1910).

At the time, the Art Nouveau movement was named differently as it began spreading from one country to another, in Spain people said "Modernismo" –referring to Antonio Gaudí (1852-1926) –, in Italy it was the "Floreale" style –with Carlo Bugatti (1856-1940) –, in Germany "Jugendstil", in Austria "Sezessionstil", at La Chaux-de-fond in Switzerland it was called "Sapin" style, in the United States "Tiffany" style, etc. However, although the movement might have had difficulties in finding a terminology that could encompass all of these groups, due to its numerous creative sources around the world, common ground could generally be found in their ideological approach. Indeed, similarly to those of Arts and Crafts, the proponents of Art Nouveau wanted to abolish all barriers between art forms, this notion greatly stimulated the decorative arts even bringing modern design to mundane household objects. To summarize, these artists all supported the concept of total artwork. This was exemplified by Victor Horta, with his Hôtel Tassel (1893, Brussels), by Henry Van de Velde and his own house, the "Bloemenwerf" (1895, Uccle), or Gaudí's buildings in Barcelona; in each case the creator was both an architect and an interior decorator, and designed every single detail from the façade to the fixtures, focusing on stylistic unity.

ANTONIO GAUDÍ
Pair of Mirrors, 1906-1910
Bevelled glass on wood,
52 × 31 × 3 cm each
Gift of Pedro and Kiki Uhart, 2002

CARLO BUGATTI
Ladie's Desk, 1890-1898
Black stained walnut, bone
inlay, incrustations of pewter,
embossed and pierced copper,
hazelnuts, goat suede leather
parchment, 134.5 × 71 × 60.5 cm
Donation of Mrs. Antonin Rispal,
2005

VICTOR HORTA
Furniture and Wood Panelling from the Hôtel Aubecq,
circa 1902-1904
Ash
Acquisition, 1980

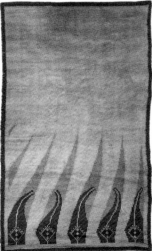

AKSELI GALLEN-KALLELA
Carpet: Flame, circa 1906
Woven wool hanging, 340 × 190 cm
Acquisition, 2006

Towards more sobriety

Rejecting excessive decorativeness as shown in the more extreme versions of Art Nouveau, several creative centres began developing a more austere formal approach, and evolving towards geometrical ornamentation. This was the case in Glasgow, Scotland, where Charles Rennie Mackintosh (1868-1928), Herbert MacNair (1868-1955) and both their wives, the Margaret sisters (1864-1933) as well as Frances MacDonald (1874-1921). In their works shapes were typically stretched vertically.

In Germany, where several major centres had emerged in Munich and Darmstadt, artists were beginning to abandon the floral Jugendstil, which continued to produce curvilinear organic style ornamentation, preferring the more austere style initiated in Germanic countries; ultimately ornamentation was dropped entirely. Peter Behrens (1868-1940) and Richard Riemerschmid (1868-1957) were among those who, early on, advocated the use of geometrical shapes. In Munich, a similar trend led to the creation of the Deutscher Werkbund, founded by Hermann Muthesius (1861-1927) in 1907; the association still upheld the presence of art in everyday life but agreed however to get involved with mechanised industrial production.

The Viennese centre illustrated in the best manner such a Functionalist purification of styles for architecture and the decorative arts. While the secessionist group, founded in 1897, was at first inspired by the curves of Art Nouveau, they rather rapidly changed perspective favouring a simplified form; a style that matured at the Wiener Werkstätte ("Viennese workshops") created in 1903 by Josef Hoffmann (1870-1956) and Koloman Moser (1868-1918). They, however, did not completely do away with ornamentation but their compatriot Adolf Loos (1870-1933) was rather more radical. In his famous 1908 essay "Ornament and Crime", Loos considers that "the evolution of culture is synonymous with the removal of ornament from objects of daily use".

All these trends announced the advent of Functionalism, a movement that was to pursue its expansion during the interwar period with the Bauhaus in Germany or Le Corbusier in France, and spread further to the United-States, namely with the Chicago School (Commercial Style) represented by such architects as Louis Sullivan (1856-1924) and Frank Lloyd Wright (1867-1959).

PETER BEHRENS
Armchair, 1901
White lacquered poplar wood, red leather seating, 106 × 65 × 45.5 cm
Acquisition with a contribution by the "Société des Amis du musée d'Orsay", 1999

JOSEPH HOFFMANN
Reclining Armchair, circa 1908
Curved beech wood, perforated plywood, mahogany coloured varnish, brass, 110 × 62 × 82 cm
Acquisition, 1986

FRANK LLOYD WRIGHT
Stained-Glass Window, circa 1908
Transparent and coloured glass, tin soldered zinc, 112 × 52 cm
Acquisition, 1986

CHARLES RENNIE MACKINTOSH
Drop-leaf Writing-Desk, circa 1904
White lacquered wood, coloured glass, steel (?), lead, silver gilded brass, 121.9 × 81.3 × 41.9 cm
Gift of Michel David-Weill through the Lutèce Foundation, 1985

KOLOMAN MOSER
Inkstand and Tray, 1905
Silver, glass, 6.7 × 9.2 × 5.5 cm and 1.5 × 22.7 × 15.4 cm
Acquisition, 1986

Dates and Events

1760-1840 **NEO-CLASSICISM**

1770-1840 **ROMANTICISM**

1836-FIN DU XIX⁰ SIÈCLE **REALISM**

1840-1870 **THE BARBIZON SCHOOL**

1874-1886 **IMPRESSIONISM**

1885-1910 **NEO-IMPRESSIONISM**

1886-1900 **SYMBOLISM**

1887-1903 **THE NABIS**

1890-1905 **ART NOUVEAU**

1848   Proclamation of the Republic; creation of the Pre-Raphaelite Brotherhood; publication of *Memoirs* by Chateaubriand (1848-1850)

1850   Scandal caused by *A Funeral at Ornans* by Gustave Courbet

1851   Coup d'état instigated by Louis-Napoleon Bonaparte; *Voyage to the Orient* by Gerard de Nerval

1852   Opening of the Bon Marché department store by Aristide Boucicaut; proclamation of the Second Empire

1853   Haussmann named Prefect of Paris: launch of the great urbanisation works in Paris

1855   Triumph of Eugène Delacroix at the Exposition Universelle in Paris

1856   Gustave Flaubert, *Madame Bovary*

1857   *The Flowers of Evil*, collection of poems by Charles Baudelaire

1858   First aerial photographs by Nadar

1859   *The Turkish Bath* by Jean-Dominique Ingres

1863   Success of *The Birth of Venus* by Antoine Cabanel at the official Salon; creation of the « Salon des refusés » and scandal caused by *The Picnic* by Édouard Manet; death of Eugène Delacroix

1865   *Olympia* by Édouard Manet; *War and Peace* published by Leon Tolstoy

1866   *La Vie parisienne*, operetta by Jacques Offenbach; *Crime and Punishment* by Dostoyevsky

1867   Exposition Universelle in Paris

1870   Fall of the Empire and proclamation of the Republic; death of Bazille

1871   Commune of Paris

1873   *A Season in Hell* by Arthur Rimbaud

1874   First Impressionist exhibition with *Impression, Rising Sun* by Claude Monet

1875   Inauguration of the new Opera House by Charles Garnier; deaths of Camille Corot and Jean-François Millet; *Carmen* by Georges Bizet

1876   Second Impressionist exhibition at the Durand-Ruel Gallery; Stéphane Mallarmé writes *Afternoon of a Faun*; Gustave Moreau, *Salomé*

1877   Death of Gustave Courbet; third Impressionist exhibition

1878   Exposition Universelle at the Trocadéro Palace: Émile Gallet receives four gold medals

1879   Fourth Impressionist exhibition

1880   Fifth Impressionist exhibition

1881   Sixth Impressionist exhibition

1882   Seventh Impressionist exhibition

1883   Construction launched for *The Sagrada Familia* by Antoni Gaudí in Barcelona; death of Édouard Manet

1884 Opening of the "Salon des Indépendants"; Paul Verlaine, *Poètes Maudits* (Accursed poets); Joris Karl Huysmans, *À rebours* (Against the grain)

1885 Paul Cézanne, *Sainte Victoire Mountain*; Émile Zola, *Germinal*; *Bel-Ami* by Guy de Maupassant

1886 Eighth and last Impressionist exhibition, with *An Afternoon at the Grande-Jatte* by Georges Seurat; inauguration of the *Statue of Liberty* by Frédéric-Auguste Bartholdi in New-York; exhibition organised by Durand-Ruel in New-York *Works, [...] by the Impressionists of Paris*

1887 Construction of the Eiffel Tower for the 1889 Exposition Universelle

1888 First showing of *The Thinker* by Auguste Rodin

1889 *Portrait of the Artist* by Vincent Van Gogh

1890 Acquisition of *Olympia* by Édouard Manet by the Luxembourg Museum thanks to a subscription launched by artists and writers; *Haystacks*, series by Claude Monet; death of Van Gogh

1891 Paul Gauguin, *Women of Tahiti*; Oscar Wilde, *The Portrait of Dorian Grey*; death of Georges Seurat

1892 Paul Signac, *Women at the Well*; Claude Debussy, *Afternoon of a Faun*

1893 Invention of the first cinematographic projector by Étienne Marey; Edvard Munch, *The Scream*

1894 Death of Gustave Caillebotte and bequeath of his collection to France

1895 Paul Cézanne, *The Bathers*; first cinematographic show by the Lumière brothers in Paris; exhibition of *Cathedrals* by Monet at the Durand-Ruel Gallery; death of Berthe Morisot

1896 First film by Georges Méliès

1897 Caillebotte bequest enters the Luxembourg Museum

1898 Launch of works for the Paris city «Métropolitain» underground train service; death of Eugène Boudin

1889 Death of Alfred Sisley

1900 Exposition Universelle; inauguration of the Orsay train station; design of the Paris «Métropolitain» entrances by Hector Guimard

1903 Deaths of Paul Gauguin and Camille Pissarro

1905 Henri Matisse, «*Luxe, calme et volupté*» (Luxurious, Peaceful and Voluptuous)

1906 Pablo Picasso, «*Les Demoiselles d'Avignon*» (Young ladies of Avignon); death of Paul Cézanne

1913 Paul Stravinsky, *The Rites of Spring*; Marcel Proust «*Du côté de chez Swann*» (Swann's Way)

1914 Beginning of the WWI

View of the Café Campana imagined by the two Brazilian designers Fernando and Humbert Campana in homage to Émile Gallé and Art Nouveau.

ORSAY MUSEUM

Guy Cogeval
President of the Orsay
and Orangerie Museums

Annie Dufour
Manager of the Publishing Department,
assisted by **Julia Hugot**

ÉDITIONS ARTLYS

Séverine Cuzin-Schulte
Editorship

Lucile Desmoulins
Editor

Catherine Enault
DTP

Pierre Kegels
Production

Graphic Arts
P&J/Laurent Pinon & Aurore Jannin

Maps
Cyrille Lebrun, Adèle Antignac and Paul Juin

Translation
Laurette Tassin

Photoengraving
Blackscan

Printer
Desbouis Grésil

ISBN : 978-2-85495-406-7

© Établissement public des musées
d'Orsay et de l'Orangerie, Paris, 2012

© Éditions Artlys, Paris, 2012

Printed at Montgeron on June, 27th 2013

Legal Deposit: July 2012

GENERAL INFORMATION

Orsay Museum
Main Entrance
1, rue de la Légion d'honneur
75007 Paris
01 40 49 48 14
www.musee-orsay.fr

OPENING HOURS

Open 9h30 à 18h00 on Tuesday, Wednesday, Friday, Saturday and Sunday;
from 9h30 to 21h45 on Thursday
Closed on Monday and on 1st January, 1st May and 25 th December

All the artworks illustrated in this catalogue belong to the Orsay Museum Collections.

Photographic credits
Orsay Museum (dist. Rmn-GP)/Sophie Boegly: back cover tl, p. 4-5, 38, 106, 114, 128; Orsay Museum (dist. Rmn-GP)/Alexis Brandt: p. 111b; Orsay Museum (dist. Rmn-GP)/D.R.: p. 7, 109t, 109b, 111t, 123t; Orsay Museum (dist. Rmn-GP)/Patrice Schmidt: back cover bl, p. 29, 33t, 33b, 34, 37, 43, 44-45, 49t, 51t, 52-53, 69b, 80-81, 85tl, 85br, 104b, 108, 110r, 112, 113t, 113b, 118l, 121t, 122l, 122d; Rmn-GP (Orsay Museum)/Daniel Arnaudet: p. 120c; Rmn-GP (Orsay Museum)/Martine Beck-Coppola: p. 75b; Rmn-GP (Orsay Museum)/Jean-Gilles Berizzi: p. 64; Rmn-GP (Orsay Museum)/Gérard Blot: back cover br, p. 46, 47t, 103, 118r, 119; Rmn-GP (Orsay Museum)/Gérard Blot/Christian Jean: p. 19t; Rmn-GP (Orsay Museum)/Gérard Blot/Hervé Lewandowski: p. 58-59; Rmn-GP (Orsay Museum)/D.R.: p. 17, 27, 125bl; Rmn-GP (Orsay Museum)/Guillot: p. 19b; Rmn-GP (Orsay Museum)/Béatrice Hatala: p. 110l; Rmn-GP (Orsay Museum)/Jean Hutin/D.R.: p. 9l; Rmn-GP (Orsay Museum)/Konstantinos Ignatiadis: p. 36c, 121b; Rmn-GP (Orsay Museum)/Christian Jean: p. 9r, 20; Rmn-GP (Orsay Museum)/Thierry Le Mage: p. 85tr; Rmn-GP (Orsay Museum)/Hervé Lewandowski: cover, back cover tr and c, p. 10, 11, 12, 13, 14, 18, 21, 23, 24, 25b, 30r, 31b, 32, 36l, 36r, 40, 41t, 41b, 42t, 42b, 47b, 48, 49b, 51b, 55t, 56, 57t, 57b, 60, 61t, 61b, 62-63, 65t, 65b, 66t, 66b, 67, 68, 69t, 70-71, 72t, 72b, 73, 74, 75t, 76t, 76b, 77, 78l, 78r, 79t, 79b, 82t, 82b, 83, 84t, 84b, 85br, 86l, 86r, 87, 88, 89, 90t, 90b, 91, 92-93, 94, 95, 96, 97t, 97b, 98-99, 100l, 100r, 101, 102, 104t, 105, 116r, 123b, 124l, 124r, 125t; Rmn-GP (Orsay Museum)/René-Gabriel Ojéda: p. 16b, 25t, 28, 31t, 116l, 117, 120l; Rmn-GP (Orsay Museum)/Thierry Ollivier: p. 26, 30l; Rmn-GP (Orsay Museum)/Franck Raux/René-Gabriel Ojéda: p. 22b; Rmn-GP (Orsay Museum)/Jean Schormans/D.R.: p. 8, 16t, 22t, 120r, 125br; Rmn-GP (Orsay Museum)/Michel Urtado: p. 50, 54, 55b.

© ADAGP, 2012 : p. 29, 30l, 33b, 36c, 96, 97b, 104t, 109t, 112, 113t, 120c, 123t, 125t, 128.